That Your Days May Be Long

Kenneth L. Gibble

faithQuest
Elgin, Illinois

That Your Days May Be Long

Kenneth L. Gibble

Copyright © 1990 by Kenneth L. Gibble

faithQuest, a division of Brethren Press, 1451 Dundee Avenue, Elgin, IL 60120

Cover design by Jeane Healey

Library of Congress Cataloguing-in-Publication Data

Gibble, Kenneth L., 1941-
    That your days may be long : a collection of plays for the
    church / Kenneth L. Gibble.
         p.   cm.
    ISBN 0-87178-841-1
    1. Christian drama, American. I. Title.
PS3557.I13916T4   1990
812'.54—DC20   90-40775
                                    CIP

Manufactured in the United States of America

Contents

This collection is dedicated to all the women and men, girls and boys, who brought these plays to life in two congregations: the Ridgeway Community Church of the Brethren, Harrisburg, Pennsylvania, and the Arlington Church of the Brethren, Arlington, Virginia.

To all the actors, directors, and behind-the-scenes specialists goes my heartfelt gratitude.

Thanks, gang!
Ken Gibble

Introduction

Why drama in the church? There are doubtless many reasons. I want to offer three.

Theology. The Bible is filled with drama. No sooner does the voice of God declare, "Let there be light," than we find ourselves caught up in the incredible three act drama of creation, judgment, and redemption. From the opening pages of Genesis with its magnificent creation story to the spectacular climax of history according to the book of Revelation, the scriptures contain scene after scene of dramatic events.

In most Christian churches, the primary means of proclaiming the gospel is that of the sermon. Despite the importance of the sermon in Christian worship, the fact remains that it is a monologue, one person speaking to many listeners. By contrast, the stories in the Bible give us the words of numerous people. Thus the presentation of a play as part of worship is more nearly in tune theologically with the scriptures than a sermon is.

Communication. Drama has a way of reaching people that simply isn't possible in a sermon. By its very definition, drama is a depiction of human interaction. What we see on stage is people facing life in much the same ways you and I face it. Whether the actors are portraying characters from the Bible or contemporary characters, we see our own struggles to believe, to endure, to find meaning, enacted in the actions in front of us. Unless the play is badly written or the acting is abominable, it is very hard to keep one's distance from a play. Watching it, we get caught up in the struggles of the characters. The boundaries between what is real and what is make-believe dissolve.

My favorite example of this phenomenon took place not long after I began my first stint as a pastor. A play I had written called for the voice of an offstage God to come booming into the dialogue. Afterwards, the father of a ten-year-old youngster told me his daughter's eyes had grown huge at the sound of "God's" voice. She whispered to her dad: "That isn't really God, is it?" Drama has the power to help us allow for what we might otherwise reject. Drama communicates by inviting us "in."

Body Building. No, not the kind of body building you accomplish by working out at the gym. The "body" to which I'm referring here is the body of Christ, otherwise known (see 1 Corinthians 12:27) as the church. People of a congregation engage in all kinds of activities: worship, pot luck dinners, volleyball games, Bible studies, the list goes on and on. But there is a special bond that develops among those who work together to do a play.

And it is work: memorizing lines, rehearsing, getting props and costumes, and maybe hardest of all, overcoming your nervousness enough to go out there on stage and risk making a fool of yourself. But from all this effort together grows a camaraderie, a mutual caring, that nothing else can match. Drama calls forth special gifts from people, the kinds of gifts Paul had in mind when he described the things that contributed to "building up the body of Christ" (Ephesians 4:12).

The plays in this book were written as chancel dramas. Most chancels have built-in limitations: no curtain, restricted space, etc. Aware of these limitations, I have kept the suggested sets as simple as possible. If you have the opportunity to present your production in another setting, you can make your staging as elaborate as your imagination will allow. Some of the plays in this book were also performed in such diverse settings as a church conference, a health care convention, a medical center classroom, and a radio studio. Feel free to adapt these dramas to whatever situation you encounter.

And don't forget to have fun!

That Your Days May Be Long

PRODUCTION NOTES

"That Your Days May Be Long" portrays a society approximately fifty years in the future. The tone of the play is somber in keeping with the kind of society in which the characters live.

The success of the play hinges on two factors: the first of which is the believability of Michael Sloan's "conversion," which itself depends on the second factor: the convincing portrayal of the old woman as, at first, an abandoned old person, and later, a loving grandmother to Mikey. The old woman's costume must be adaptable to the suggested age change. A shawl worn over her head at first could later be dropped to her shoulders or discarded.

The other characters, except for Mikey, should wear clothes that suggest a controlled, regimented society. Bright colors should be avoided. The set should feature a conference table with chairs. Other pops needed include briefcases, pens, clipboards, manuscripts and other items suggested by the script.

Suggested scripture text: Exodus 20:12 and Matthew 15:1-9

CAST

MICHAEL SLOAN	About 40, serous-minded, new to political maneuvering. Along among the major characters, he experiences a conversion of sorts.
DAPHE CARNES	in her 30s or 40s, bright, outspoken, determined.
GEORGE HARDING	Late 40s or older, a seasoned veteran of political dealings.
MARY MCCLAIN	Non-speaking role of an officious secretary.
KATHERINE DANIELS	Ph.D., social scientist, distinguished career in research at National University.
PETER KRAVEK	Psychiatrist and specialist in psychological disorders of venerable. Ally of George Harding.
OLD WOMAN	In her first appearance, a woman of 75 plus years. At the end of the play, she is younger, in her early 60s.
CHILD	Mikey, a boy of about 10.

(Michael Sloan and Daphne Carnes enter together, carrying small briefcases, place them on table and remain standing during their conversation.)

DAPHNE CARNES: Tell me, Michael... is it all right if I call you Michael?... were you surprised in being named to the panel?

MICHAEL SLOAN: Yeah, kind of. It's really strange; there are certainly other people, like yourself, who have lots more experience in this kind of thing. I'm a teacher and a writer, not a social engineer.

DAPHNE CARNES: Don't sell yourself short. I've read some of your articles. You're a very bright guy, and your piece in New Vistas magazine on the need to upgrade environmental conditions in the security areas for venerables was brilliant.

MICHAEL SLOAN: *(A bit embarrassed by the praise)* Well... thank you, uh, Daphne. It's probably that article that got me appointed to this study panel. In your case, though, it was surely no surprise to anyone. I mean, you're probably the foremost authority in care for venerables in the country.

DAPHNE CARNES: *(laughs)* I'm just enough of an egotist to enjoy hearing you say that. *(getting serious)* I am hoping I can count on your support when we consider the new programs that are so necessary. I know we will catch a lot of flak from the bleeding hearts who'd like to turn back the clock. *(lowers voice conspiratorially)* Just between us, I think George Harding was a terrible choice to head the panel. Of the three of us, he's obviously the least competent. Let's face it; he got his assignment for political reasons. That means he won't want to make waves. But I think we've got to advocate strong, decisive measures. Our job is to do the best for society as a whole, even if some individuals do have to make some sacrifices. Don't you agree?

MICHAEL SLOAN: Well, yes... I... I guess so. Only...
(George Harding enters and walks briskly over to Daphne Carnes.)

GEORGE HARDING: Daphne, how good to see you again. I'm sure we won't lack for strong opinions with you on the panel.

DAPHNE CARNES: *(With some sarcasm)* Why George, how sweet of you to say so. George Harding, meet Michael Sloan. Michael, this is George.

MICHAEL SLOAN: Believe me, Magistrate Harding, it's a real privilege to...

GEORGE HARDING: No, no, just "George" is fine. I like to keep things on an informal basis. I've admired your writings.

MICHAEL SLOAN: *(pleased)* You read my article in New Vistas.

GEORGE HARDING: Well... no, I've not actually read your work, but I have heard good things about it.

MICHAEL SLOAN: Oh.

GEORGE HARDING: Well, now that we've cared for the amenities, we might as well get started. My secretary should be along any minute now, and... here she comes now. *(enter Mary McClain)* Mary, you can sit here and the rest of us can use the table. *(Group moves to table and gets out papers, pencils, etc.)* Now, just to review what our assignment is... we've been appointed as a panel of three to conduct hearings and make recommendations for more efficient and humane care for the venerables. I don't suppose I need to underline the fact that the new Administration is hoping for some creative thinking from us. The problem of the venerables, of course, can be political dynamite if it isn't handled carefully. Naturally, we'll need to present a united front on this. It wouldn't do to give the critics a chance to make waves.

DAPHNE CARNES: *(sarcastically, with a knowing glance at Michael)* Oh, of course not, there mustn't be any waves.

GEORGE HARDING: Good. I hope you'll both be willing to be the team players the Administration is counting on. Okay, any questions before we call in the first person for testimony?

MICHAEL SLOAN: Uh, George, just one thing. I'm a bit new at this game. Will our recommendations carry much weight?

DAPHNE CARNES: *(laughs cynically)* My dear Michael, you are an innocent! The Assembly has to vote on what we recommend, of course, but that's just a formality. *(grows more and more intense)* No, we are the ones with the power now. With Administration backing, what we propose will shape the future for the next ten generations! That's why it is imperative that we act decisively. If we fail, the problems of the venerables could destroy our society.

GEORGE HARDING: *(drily)* That may be putting it a little strong, Daphne.

DAPHNE CARNES: No, George. On the contrary, I haven't stated it strongly enough! Your trouble is a near-sighted view of reality all done in the name of political expediency.

GEORGE HARDING: And your trouble is the unwillingness to consider the slightest possibility that you might, just once, be wrong!

MICHAEL SLOAN: Uh, maybe we ought to call in the first expert.

(George and Daphne continue to glare at each other for a moment.)

GEORGE HARDING: *(recovering)*

You're right, Michael. Mary, would you ask Dr. Daniels to come in. Let's see, *(reading)* Katherine Daniels, Ph.D, social scientist, distinguished career in research at National University, et cetera, et cetera...

DAPHNE CARNES: Yes, George, we know all about the eminent Doctor Daniels. Some of us here do our homework.

(enter Katherine Daniels, followed by Mary)

GEORGE HARDING: *(rising, as others rise)* Dr. Daniels, it's so good of you to join us. My colleagues, Michael Sloan and Daphne Carnes.

KATHERINE DANIELS: Thank you. I'm grateful for the invitation to testify.

GEORGE HARDING: Not at all. Why don't you proceed.

KATHERINE DANIELS: As you can see on the documents I've prepared for your study, I've given a detailed history of care of the venerables in the past century. Let me summarize what I've written in a few broad strokes. You know, of course, that the venerable population first began to be a problem in the latter half of the previous century. At that time, the median age in the country had begun to inch upward. Couples were having fewer children, some were deciding not to have children at all. Medical advances extended life expectancy. Up till then, financial support of the venerables, who were known at that time as "senior citizens" or "the elderly," came from a program called *(checks notes)* "Social Security." As that system neared bankruptcy, benefits were reduced. That was merely the first step in a more realistic approach to the problem.

DAPHNE CARNES: Excuse me, Dr. Daniels, but in this report you state that the introduction of Venerable Security Centers came in 1998. I believe a more careful check of the records will reveal that the first center was opened in September of the preceding year.

KATHERINE DANIELS: *(icily)* Thank you. I'll double check on that.

GEORGE HARDING: While we've paused for a moment, Dr. Daniels, refresh my memory on why and when the term "venerables" was first used.

KATHERINE DANIELS: Of course.When the Security Center idea was first proposed, there were protests from many quarters that placing all people over 70 in restricted areas was inhumane and a denial of their rights. In rebuttal, the government pointed out the necessity of protecting the elderly against attacks by hoodlums in the cities and elsewhere. Bringing them together in Security Centers also offered an end to their loneliness and neglect. And as a way of underlining its high regard for old people, the Administration then in power used the word "venerables," which means "people held in great esteem." With the establishment of Venerable Security Centers, the term "venerables" soon was being used by everyone.

DAPHNE CARNES: It was a stroke of genius. It shifted the attention away from what was the real issue: forced removal of the venerable population to the Security Centers. That's the kind of creative thinking called for now.

GEORGE HARDING: Yes, well. Please proceed, Dr. Daniels.

KATHERINE DANIELS: Thank you. To continue: after theSecurity Centers were first opened in either '97 or '98 *(gives fierce look at Daphne)*, other enlightened programs followed. Because the venerables all lived together, activities of special interest and benefit to venerables could more easily be organized. Medical care was centralized and streamlined. Soon after the turn of the century, of course, voluntary termination was initiated.

GEORGE HARDING: I'm curious on one point there. Historically there were strong sentiments in opposition to euthanasia, or "mercy-killing" as it was once called. How was this prejudice overcome?

MICHAEL SLOAN: Maybe I can speak to that. Some of my historical research was in that area. A strong campaign was begun to demonstrate to the venerables that voluntary termination was actually a highly moral act, in that it placed the good of society above their own welfare. There was strong opposition to this practice for a time, just as there was at first to abortion, but eventually common sense prevailed.

GEORGE HARDING: *(with admiration)* Thank you, Michael. That was helpful.

DAPHNE CARNES: Dr. Daniels, your demographic section puzzles me somewhat. I refer in particular to the graph on page 63 of your report. *(Enter old woman slowly, leaning on a cane, takes a seat, keeps head bowed. Michael sees her, is made uncomfortable because no one else seems to notice, finally interrupts).* Your data would indicate that up to the year 2011, there was little significant change in the median age of venerables, particularly females. However, my own study, which appears incidentally...

MICHAEL SLOAN: Uh... excuse me, Daphne, but...

DAPHNE CARNES: Yes?

GEORGE HARDING: What is it, Michael?

MICHAEL SLOAN: Well, I mean... that venerable there...that woman. Shouldn't someone see what... *(stands)*

GEORGE HARDING: Woman? Where? *(looks around)*

DAPHNE CARNES: Aren't you feeling well, Michael?

MICHAEL SLOAN: I... I... don't know. I...

GEORGE HARDING: Mary, go get Michael a glass of water. *(Gets up and goes to Michael, lays a hand on his shoulder)* Just relax, Michael. Look, are you okay or should we take a break?

MICHAEL SLOAN: No, no, I'm all right.

GEORGE HARDING: Are you sure?

MICHAEL SLOAN: Yes. I've... I've been under a bit of a strain lately... But... I'll be fine. *(Sits down and looks at old woman. Everyone on stage freezes in position as old woman rises and intones her lines.)*

OLD WOMAN: "Honor your father and your mother, that your days may be long in the land which the Lord your God gives you." *(exit old woman)*

GEORGE HARDING: Well then, Dr. Daniels, we appreciate your report. We will need time to study it and we may well call you in for another session. *(George and Katherine rise)*

KATHERINE DANIELS: I'm glad to be of assistance. Thank you. *(Mary shows Katherine out.)*

GEORGE HARDING: All right. Next will be Peter Kravek, M.D., psychiatrist and specialist in psychological disorders in venerables. And, I might add, a personal friend. *(Enter Peter Kravek. Others stand.)* Pete, how good to see you. *(They exchange handshake.)* My colleagues, Daphne Carnes and Michael Sloan.

PETER KRAVEK: Delighted to meet you both. *(All are seated.)*

DAPHNE CARNES: Dr. Kravek, I'll get right to the point. We anticipate criticism of our proposal to begin a program of "limited involuntary termination" and I underscore the word "limited" for venerables. These critics will claim that the mental anguish caused to venerables would be inhumane. What is your opinion?

PETER KRAVEK: In my report on page 38, I address this issue; let me read...

DAPHNE CARNES: But in your own words, Doctor.

PETER KRAVEK: *(Glances with some worry at George)* **Well,** it is true that at first there will be some of the venerables who will have trouble adjusting. After all, our policy up till now has been that all terminations were strictly voluntary. Once the new policy is made public, there are bound to be some people upset. That's why I favor a more moderate course. At the beginning...

DAPHNE CARNES: Yes, I know all about your "moderate course," Doctor. Like George here, you want to restrict terminations to the most extreme cases of physical and mental disability. You think you can convince the public that, after all, it's a kindness to put them out of their misery, much like shooting a horse with a broken leg.

PETER KRAVEK: Well, I really don't...

DAPHNE CARNES: What I propose is more honest, and in the long run, less cruel. We all agree that it is no longer economically feasible to support the large venerable population. They are a dead weight on our social order; they produce nothing, yet require an enormous amount of care. Our ultimate aim is to reduce the number of venerables to a minimum. Right?

GEORGE HARDING
AND PETER KRAVEK: Yes...but...

DAPHNE CARNES: All right then. Let's stop pretending otherwise. It's time we bite the bullet and call for the radical measures we really need. Don't you agree, Michael?

MICHAEL SLOAN: Well, I must say, Daphne, that your approach does seem logical. Why not lay the whole thing out at once and get the battle

over with? To drag it out over a long period is less humane in some ways then...
(Breaks off and stares as old woman enters. Other characters freeze.)

OLD WOMAN:
My way of life
Is fallen into the sear, the yellow leaf.
And that which should accompany old age,
As honor, love, obedience, troops of friends,
I must not look to have; but in their stead,
Curses not loud, but deep, mouth-honor breath,
Which the poor heart would fain deny,
and dare not.

(Old woman is seated. Group resumes dialogue unchanged, except for Michael, who continues staring at old woman.)

PETER KRAVEK:
I think we need to be practical here. From a psychological standpoint, we are going to have a real problem on our hands when the categories of those eligible for termination are made public. Not just among the venerables, but with those nearing venerable status and even among the general population.

GEORGE HARDING:
Let's look at the proposed categories again. *(Hands a paper to Michael)* Michael... uh... Michael.

MICHAEL SLOAN:
(Distractedly) Yes?

GEORGE HARDING:
Here is your copy of the category list Daphne has outlined.

MICHAEL SLOAN:
Oh... yes.

GEORGE HARDING:
Now Category One we have no quarrel about. This includes all who are in advanced stages of senility, or who have a terminal illness. Incidentally, is the usual method of intravenous administration to be followed for termination in all categories, Peter?

PETER KRAVEK:	Yes. It has worked well with voluntary termination and we see no problem with those who will not offer any... ah... resistance. With those in the higher categories, of course, preliminary doses of medication might be necessary.
DAPHNE CARNES:	Category Two should present no problem. It includes those in earlier stages of senility, as well as those who score below the 25th percentile in the Morton/Rinehart Intelligence Tests. The Third Category: those who require more than thirty hours of nursing care a month, plus all non-ambulatories, as well as the blind and deaf. The Fourth Category is, of course, the most controversial. It includes all who have no living children, plus those whose children have signed a consent form for termination of their parents.
GEORGE HARDING:	Daphne, there is no way on God's green earth we're going to push that one through. What's left of the religious community and civil liberties groups will scream bloody murder.
DAPHNE CARNES:	Michael is more familiar with that sector than any of us, I believe. He's followed their statements in his research and... weren't you at one time in training for the priesthood, Michael?
MICHAEL SLOAN:	*(embarrassed)* Oh... yes... well, that was long ago. I was very young. *(Lapses into silence as he stares at old woman)*
GEORGE HARDING:	Michael?
MICHAEL SLOAN:	Oh yes... I was very young. And... and idealistic. But, uh... the churches. Well, they will protest, a few of them anyway. But the leaders are more enlightened on these matters now. They see the necessity of supporting Administration policies in return for certain... ah... considerations.

You know, tax exemptions, et cetera, et cetera. On the moral issue... Well, there was resistance for a time to enforced sterilization and later to mandated abortions when they were first proposed. But their theologians found a way to justify it on the basis of what they labeled "the higher morality." It was much the same as the traditional "just war" theory, which permitted killing of the enemy under certain conditions. Capital punishment, of course, was another socially approved form of termination supported by many in the religious community. So when voluntary termination of venerables began, the churches had little left to stand on by way of objection. I think we can anticipate a few indignant cries of moral outrage from some radicals, but little in the way of organized opposition.

(Child enters and sits at feet of old woman. All but Michael freeze in position.)

CHILD: Grandma, are you old?

OLD WOMAN: *(Becomes human, warm, alive)* Am I old? *(laughs)* Well, I guess so. I'm older than you are, Mikey, that's for sure. But what makes you ask that?

CHILD: Well, Marsha—she lives next door—told me that when people get old they are called venerables and have to go away somewhere to live.

OLD WOMAN: She's right about that. But I'll still live here for a few years, and even when I have to move... well, you'll be older then.

CHILD: But I'll still be able to come and see you, won't I?

OLD WOMAN: Oh yes. If you want to.

CHILD: I'll always want to.

OLD WOMAN: *(teasing)*

Just so you'll be able to eat my blueberry pies.

CHILD: *(laughing)* I hope you'll still make them. *(pause)* Grandma, what happens to people when they get real, real old?

OLD WOMAN: Well, Mikey, when they are real, real old, they get sick and die. We all have to die sometime.

CHILD: I hope it's a long, long time before you die, Grandma. *(He gets up and she pulls him to her in an embrace.)*

OLD WOMAN: Me too, Mikey. Me too. *(They exit together, old woman leaves cane behind and walks out as a younger woman would. Michael is left staring open-mouthed as they exit.)*

GEORGE HARDING: Thank you for that run-down, Michael. Michael? *(Looks at others in bewilderment)* Michael!

MICHAEL SLOAN: *(Still dazed, mutters mostly to himself)* Me too, Grandma.

DAPHNE CARNES: *(sharply)* Dr. Sloan!

MICHAEL SLOAN: *(Pulls himself back to the present)* Yes... Uh... Where was I?

DAPHNE CARNES: That's a good question, Doctor. Where were you? We are discussing important proposals for care of venerables. Remember?

PETER KRAVEK: Obviously Dr. Sloan isn't himself today. There's really no need...

DAPHNE CARNES: What there is need for, Dr. Kravek, is careful attention to these proposals. We can't afford to have any of us spaced out half the time.

GEORGE HARDING: That will do! I'm in charge, Daphne, not you. You seem to keep forgetting that. Now I suggest we get back to the business at hand. Peter, thank you for coming. We will study your report and give careful attention to your recommendations.

PETER KRAVEK: Thank you. Good luck to all of you. *(Gets up and leaves rather hastily)*

GEORGE HARDING: *(soothingly)* Michael, are you ready to continue, or should we dismiss until after lunch?

MICHAEL SLOAN: No. I'm all right... now.

GEORGE HARDING: Good. Now as I see it, we need a compromise of sorts. What it boils down to is that we all favor the proposal calling for termination of those in Category One and possibly Two. Dr. Carnes wants those in Categories Three and Four included also. She and I disagree there. So, Michael, it looks as if you are going to be the tie-breaker here. How do you stand?

MICHAEL SLOAN: Where will it end?

GEORGE HARDING: I beg your pardon?

MICHAEL SLOAN: I said, where will it end? We've come a long way in social engineering, thanks to people like you, Magistrate, and you, Dr. Carnes. And, I suppose, even to me. We've eliminated nearly all the undesirables in society. We will soon have achieved a Utopia of sorts; the Kingdom of God on earth, was what they once called it. Except none of us here believes in God, of course.

DAPHNE CARNES: Dr. Sloan, what are...

MICHAEL SLOAN: First it was hardened criminals; they were expendable. Then it was unwanted pregnancies, then it was malformed and severely retarded children, then old people were invited to volunteer for "termination." Actually, we meant "suicide," but we couldn't call it that, of course.

23

GEORGE HARDING:	Michael, I thought you were a team player. The Administration needs people who will play ball...
MICHAEL SLOAN:	Play ball, Magistrate! An excellent choice of words. This is rather like a game, isn't it? Only it's not a ball game. It's more like a chess board, with all kinds of figures in front of us, and you and I sit and decide who will survive and who will be sacrificed. There's only one thing. It isn't wooden figures we're dealing with; it's people, flesh and blood people. And it isn't "termination" we're proposing at all. Let's call it what it really is: murder!
DAPHNE CARNES:	George, I think this has gone on long enough. I move we adjourn.
MICHAEL SLOAN:	Oh no, Dr. Carnes. Don't worry. I'm not going to do anything rash. I've spent my whole life rationalizing about the work I do, about the compromises I've had to make. I've learned how to "play ball" as Magistrate Harding so fittingly puts it. I'm not dangerous. You are the dangerous ones: cold, calculating. I always thought that's what I wanted to be too. *(Gets up and speaks mostly to himself)* You know, I hadn't thought about my grandmother for years. She died, you know, when I was 12. In one of the first Venerable Security Centers. Of natural causes. At least, that's what we were told...
GEORGE HARDING:	Yes, Daphne. I think you're right. It is time to adjourn. Under the circumstances, Dr. Sloan, I must tell you that I will recommend a replacement for you on the panel. You understand, of course?
MICHAEL SLOAN:	Oh yes. I understand all right. But tell me, Magistrate. Just one question. How old are you? Never mind. Don't answer that. Let me go back to my original question, one even you can't answer: "where will it

end?" Who will be the next group to be "terminated"? People with brown skin, weak chins, red hair? Or maybe people who don't or can't play ball any longer. People who... *(Gestures with right arm as he leaves)*... make waves.

Pharaoh Decides

PRODUCTION NOTES

The action of the play occurs two days after the first-born sons of Egypt have died. Although the daughter of Pharaoh introduces the play, it would be helpful to have a worship leader read the scripture text before the play begins. Costuming can be done to suggest the time in which the action takes place. A white dress for Pharaoh's daughter, a robe for the priest, and loose-fitting garments for Setimose and Pharaoh will suffice.

Suggested scripture test: Exodus 12:29-32; 14:5-9, 26-31

That; Your, Days May Be Long

CAST

(Pharaoh's daughter enters and stands upstage left. She speaks directly to the audience.)

PHARAOH'S DAUGHTER: My father is a stubborn man. Being the Pharaoh, the ruler of a powerful nation makes it difficult to be anything else, I suppose. But I think my father would have been just as stubborn had he been born a slave. I know my father loves me. And I suspect, though he would never admit it, that I was his favorite. I say he would never admit it because that is something a Pharaoh cannot say. The first-born son is the heir to the throne, and all Egypt must be made to believe that the Pharaoh loves above everyone else the son who will succeed him to the throne. And so all Egypt now mourns. Not just because the god of Moses has slain our firstborn sons, but because my brother, the next Pharaoh, is dead. Our future has been stolen from us. I cannot speak to anyone of my own grief. I have lost not only a brother, but a son. Though in another sense, I lost my son long ago. What a lovely child he was, the baby I found floating in a basket among the river reeds. And what a fine specimen of a man Moses turned out to be. But he left us. I thought I would never see him again. What a shock when he returned to champion the cause of the Hebrew slaves. I was forbidden to be present when he came to speak with Pharaoh. But I watched him from a distance. I cannot describe the feelings I had when I saw him after so many years. And now he is gone again; he and his people have left Egypt singing praises to their god for deliverance. We shall see. There are those who wish to bring them back. As a woman I can have no part in such decisions. But watch and listen. My uncle and the high priest are both waiting to talk to my father.

(Setimose enters. He paces for several moments, glancing towards the entrance from time to time. He is obviously waiting for someone. Tutamon enters and greets Setimose with a curt nod of his head.)

TUTAMON: So you're here ahead of me this time. I know it is said one has to get up early to outsmart the high priest, but this is the first time the Pharaoh's brother has done it.

SETIMOSE: If it takes an early rising to outsmart another, then apparently the Hebrews' god rises earlier than the gods of the Egyptians. Or does the great high priest of Amon-Ra have a better explanation?

TUTAMON: Take care, Setimose. When the gods have disposed of the Hebrews, they may turn their attention to those who dare to blaspheme, even if one of them is the brother of Pharaoh.

SETIMOSE: *(With a cold smile)* Well, Tutamon, I see these grim events have unsettled you. Usually you allow others to make your threats for you. But why should we stand here quarreling so early in the morning? I've been waiting for you to arrive. I think it would be wise if we chatted a bit before going in to see my brother.

TUTAMON: What have we to talk about?

SETIMOSE: *(Turns his back on Tutamon and thinks for a moment. When he faces Tutamon again, his face and voice are solemn.)* I was hoping I might convince you to soften your position a little. *(Tutamon tries to interrupt, but Setimose holds up his hand, palm outward)* No, wait. I know we are old enemies. I don't expect that to change. But now that the Hebrews have left, there is at least some chance we can get back to normal again. Look, Tutamon, we both know why you were sent for. My brother is a troubled man. He's vain and indecisive. The horror of his son's death, of all the deaths, drove him to his knees. I was present when he called in Moses and Aaron and Miriam and ordered them to leave Egypt with their people. I have never seen him so distraught. He even begged them to give him their god's blessing before he left. But now, typically, he's having second thoughts. He's wondering: maybe we ought to fetch the Hebrews back. He wants you here to reinforce that opinion.

TUTAMON: And that is exactly what I intend to do.

SETIMOSE: But haven't we suffered enough already? I'm not just talking now about the flies, the locusts, and all the other plagues we've endured. Not even the night of cataclysm. I mean that this whole controversy is tearing us apart. Already I've heard that some of the nobles are planning to petition Pharaoh to send the army to round up the Hebrews and bring them back. Others are convinced that the Hebrews' god will continue to afflict us so long as the Hebrews remain on Egyptian soil.

TUTAMON: (With a sneer) Are you convinced of that yourself, Setimose? Has Moses and his tricks persuaded you to be a worshiper of Yahweh?

SETIMOSE: Don't be ridiculous. I leave theology to you priests.

TUTAMON: Then perhaps you will understand why this priest will tell Pharaoh that the Hebrews must be rounded up and brought back. I may even tell him it is an act of charity to do so. Without food they will perish in a few weeks. I don't expect Pharaoh to understand the religious significance of this whole business, anymore than I expect you to understand. For you, it is of little consequence that the god of the Hebrews now can claim a victory over the godhead

Amon-Ra. You and I may see all this as superstitious nonsense, but once the Egyptian people lose confidence in our gods, our society will begin to unravel. They will call into question everything, even the authority of the aristocracy and the Pharaoh ...

SETIMOSE: To say nothing of the high priest!

TUTAMON: *(infuriated)* I think there is no further point in continuing this conversation. I suggest we do what we came to do ... speak with Pharaoh. *(They exit)*

PHARAOH'S DAUGHTER: You see how it is, don't you? How much depends on what my father decides. It is treason to say it, of course, but I hope Moses and his people make good their escape. What I fear is more bloodshed, more death. I have said my father is stubborn. But so is Moses, and so, it would seem, is the god of the Hebrews.

(Stage is set to suggest Pharaoh's quarters. A table contains wine and goblets and a board game. Three chairs are needed. Pharaoh enters and pulls a chair up to the table. He rolls dice, moves tokens on the board, takes a drink of wine. He hums to himself and betrays that he is slightly drunk. Enter Setimose and Tutamon.)

PHARAOH: Ah, my two most valuable counselors, his priestly eminence Tutamon, and my royal brother Setimose. Sit, gentlemen, sit. Have some wine, gentlemen. A very good year, this vintage. A very good year indeed. *(His hand trembles as he takes another drink.)* Yes, yes, I know. Rumor has it that I drink wine only on ceremonial occasions, and that when I just want to get tiddly, like now, I prefer good old barley beer, like any common swillbelly farmer. *(Leans toward them conspiratorially.)* Well, let me tell you, straight from the horse's mouth ...

what they say is absolutely, positively true!

TUTAMON: *(After an awkward pause)* Pharaoh, I think the Hebrew slaves must be brought back at once. The gods of Egypt are offended by the pretensions of the Hebrew god.

PHARAOH: Oh horsecookies, Tutamon. You don't believe that stuff anymore than I do. Let's cut through all the garbage and get to the bottom line. I've called you both in because you are the two most powerful men in Egypt, next to my own hallowed person, of course. I've also called you in because you hate each other, and I've learned that the energy of two hatreds matched against each other clears my mind, helps me decide what to do.

SETIMOSE: Egypt is well rid of the Hebrews, Pharaoh. Let Moses lead them to starvation in the wilderness, if it comes to that. They and their god have brought us nothing but misery.

PHARAOH: *(After a pause, he speaks in a dreamlike voice.)* I remember the first time I saw him, a helpless baby that my daughter brought to me. I am adopting him as my son, she said. She didn't ask me; she told me. Like so many things where my daughter was concerned, I had no choice in the matter. What will you name him? I said. Moses, she told me. How much later was it that I learned he was one of them, the son of slaves? And then when he grew up he fled to the desert. Why? I wondered. And when he and his brother and sister came for an audience, I didn't know him at first. It was only when he stammered in his speech that I recognized him. That, and the way he carried himself. Everyone wondered where a slave could have learned such bearing, such presence. But I knew. He learned it here, in Pharaoh's palace. And there was something else, a power to him that one doesn't learn even if you are grandson to Pharaoh. When I asked him about that power, he said it was the power of Yahweh in him. I laughed at him.

TUTAMON: Pharaoh, give the order. Send your army after them. The reconnaissance reports indicate they've turned toward the sea. Our troops could round them up like cattle and have them back in a day.

PHARAOH: Yes, I suppose we could.

TUTAMON: Pharaoh, it can be done; therefore it should be done!

PHARAOH: (Turns to face Setimose) Brother, you are strangely silent. Is it the earliness of the hour or your usual cold disapproval of my drinking that holds your tongue? I've always envied your ability to look danger squarely in the face. But I sense that the horror that has come upon us has dented even your armor. Is that so?

SETIMOSE: It is, Pharaoh.

PHARAOH: So you think we should leave well enough alone? But, brother, many of noble birth in Egypt are already clamoring for me to do as the high priest says. They say the loss of the Hebrew slaves will ruin the economy, will destroy the nation. They say that giving in to a race of slaves betrays a fatal weakness on our part. How do I answer that?

SETIMOSE: The Hebrews told us that Yahweh was a god of justice and freedom. Once having a taste of that freedom, do you think they will come back to slavery? Many will die rather than submit to that. Do you want their blood on your hands? And if Yahweh is indeed a god of justice and freedom, isn't it pointless to resist?

TUTAMON: And what kind of god would choose a miserable bunch of slaves to worship him? Such a god is a joke!

PHARAOH: *(Gestures for Tutamon to be silent)* What else, Setimose?

SETIMOSE: My brother, the Pharaohs of Egypt are remembered for many things. Their tombs testify to their power, their wealth, their accomplishments, their honor. What do you wish to be remembered for? Will generations to come be able to say that Ramses was an honorable, just Pharaoh, a ruler who kept his solemn word even to a slave people?

TUTAMON: Stop talking nonsense! History never asks: were you right, were you just? History asks one question and one question only: did you win? Pharaoh, you have the power to bring back the Hebrews. In the name of all the gods, use it!

PHARAOH: *(He pauses to take another drink, then turns to Setimose.)* Setimose, your arguments are eloquent. I am moved by them. The high priest's arguments are compelling. I am persuaded by them. I have made my decision. Let us see what the Hebrews' god will do when Pharaoh's chariots roll towards the sea.

After the Whale

PRODUCTION NOTES

"Jonah and the whale" has always been a favorite of children and grown-ups alike. This version of the story concentrates primarily on what happened to Jonah "after the whale," when he finally reaches Nineveh.

The set for the play can be as simple as one large rock (or something that looks like a large rock) on a bare stage. The only props needed are a stepladder, a paper sun, and a paper or cardboard plant for the Stage Manager to carry.

Costuming for the Stage Manager should be casual clothing such as jeans and tee shirt. The Ninevite should be attired in something to suggest the Biblical "sackcloth and ashes," old clothing streaked with real ashes or charcoal will do fine. Jonah should wear severe clothing to suggest a stereotypical fire and brimstone preacher, perhaps a dark suit with a white shirt and black tie or clerical collar. Jonah might even come on stage clutching a Bible to his chest.

The Stage Manager's speeches should be delivered in a breezy, conversational style. The Ninevite can be alternatively playful and sincere with Jonah. Jonah's mood will be unremittingly dark throughout the play until his very last line.

Suggested scripture text: Jonah 1:1-3

CAST

STAGE MANAGER

THE NINEVITE

JONAH

STAGE MANAGER: *(Enters from right, carrying ladder and paper sun, crosses stage, sets up ladder, and as he/she is about to ascend the ladder, turns and notices audience)* Oh, hello. Don't mind me. I've got to paste this piece of paper to the wall. So, just go on with whatever you were doing. *(Tries vainly to stick the "sun" to the wall)* Come on, sun. We've got to have you shining up here in the heavens or there won't be any play. *(Finally gives up, comes down and props sun against ladder)* Well, that's just going to have to be good enough. You won't mind, will you? I mean you can pretend that's the sun up in the sky, just as well as if it were up there on the wall. Actually, the sun plays a very important part in the play, so we have to put it somewhere.

Don't know why I'm telling you all this, but I'm glad to talk to somebody about this production. To tell the truth, I'm not very happy about the play itself and especially about the director. I was asked if I'd be part of this play about Jonah, see. So I say, "Great, I think I'd like to portray Jonah."

"Well," says the director, "we already have someone lined up for the part of Jonah." So that got me to thinking, and the only other character I could remember from the story was ... the whale! And I wasn't too thrilled about the idea of spouting up water from the middle of my back. Well, to make a long story short, the director had something else in mind for me, stage manager, to be exact. Big deal! About the only good thing I can say for the whole project is that it got me to read the book of Jonah in the Old Testament.

All I remembered from Sunday school days was Jonah getting swallowed and coughed up again three days later. Turns out, though, that the whale bit was a minor part of the story. Anyhow, the Bible says it was a great fish, rather than a whale, that did the swallowing ... not that it makes any big difference. I find that part of the story pretty hard to swallow anyway. *(Gives a nasty grin at this terrible pun)*

But you see, the Lord God tells Jonah to go to the wicked city of Nineveh and tell those terrible people that their sins have come to the attention of the Almighty. Jonah feels about his assignment a little like I do about my assignment in this play; in other words, he isn't exactly thrilled. So he hops on a ship sailing in the opposite direction. A storm comes up; the sailors discover that Jonah is the cause of the storm and heave him overboard.

And here's where the whale part comes in, remember? Jonah gets carried by the whale to land. And no sooner does he get on shore than the Lord reassigns him to the Nineveh preaching mission. Well, Jonah has had it with rough voyages and being swallowed and all so he sets out for Nineveh where he preaches fire and brimstone from one end of the city to the other. Fact is, he probably takes out some of his frustrations in his sermons. Some preachers have a reputation for doing that.

"Forty days," he tells them, "and then the Lord will destroy the city." Well, much to Jonah's surprise–and maybe the Lord's too–the people of Nineveh repent of their sins. They put on sackcloth and ashes, they fast and ask God to forgive them. So the Lord decides not to destroy the city ... and ... uh oh, here comes the cast. I've got to go. Be seeing you later. *(Exit)*

(Enter Jonah who takes a seat on the "rock." He faces the audience, his expression one of brooding anger)

NINEVITE: *(Enters, dressed in sackcloth and ashes)* Hello there. Why, I believe you're Jonah, the great prophet, aren't you? *(Jonah continues to stare ahead gloomily)*

Sure, you're Jonah, all right. Gosh, I never expected to meet you way out here. You must be enjoying the view. You certainly do get a beautiful view of our city from here, right? *(Jonah makes no response)*

Uh huh. Not much of a conversationalist. Some preacher though. You put the fear into this town like no one ever did. *(Gazes in the direction of Nineveh)* Oh yes, this is a fine view. That is one beautiful city down there.

JONAH: I think it's ugly.

NINEVITE: Oh, you do talk. But how in heaven's name can you call Nineveh ugly? Look at the beautiful white roofs gleaming in the sun.

JONAH: Don't even mention the sun. It's so hot I can hardly stand it.

NINEVITE: Sorry, I guess you're not used to this warm climate. It must be cooler back where you live. By the way, where do you come from?

JONAH: Jerusalem.

NINEVITE: Jerusalem? Is that a town, a country, a mountain?

JONAH: *(Indignantly)* Jerusalem is Zion, the dwelling place of the Most High God. It is a city set on a hill, fairer than a thousand of your Ninevehs.

NINEVITE: Sounds like quite a place. And it must be quite a way from here too. How did you get here, by ship?

JONAH: By whale.

NINEVITE: By what?

JONAH: Never mind. It's a long story. *(Pause while Ninevite finds a place to sit down)*

NINEVITE: Tell me, Jonah, do you really think the Lord God will destroy our lovely city?

JONAH: *(Begins in a low voice and then gradually builds to a deafening climax, complete with appropriate stalking back and forth and wild arm gestures)* And why not? It's a city filled with the worst wickedness in the world. The evil in Nineveh is an abomination in the eyes of the Lord of Hosts. The Lord abhors your sinful ways, your profane worship of idols. Woe to the city soaked in blood, full of lies, stuffed with booty, whose plunderings know no end. The day of the Lord will come upon this city.

A day of wrath, that day,
a day of distress and agony,
a day of ruin and devastation,
a day of darkness and gloom,
a day of cloud and blackness.

You will be driven away like chaff that is blown away in a day. The wrath of the Lord will descend upon you. You will be utterly destroyed.

NINEVITE: *(wryly)* Well, I guess that answers my question.

JONAH: I have come to this hillside to await with pleasure the devastation of Nineveh.

NINEVITE: But what about all the repentance the people have made for their sins? Everybody has been praying and fasting for weeks. From the least to the greatest, they've all turned from their wickedness and asked for God's forgiveness. I mean even the politicians have become honest. And look at this get-up. Do you think we're all wearing this sackcloth and ashes because it's the latest fashion?

JONAH: *(Looks at Ninevite for the first time)* I hadn't noticed. Well, it won't do you any good. You all deserve to be utterly destroyed.

NINEVITE: I don't get it. Wasn't the whole point of your coming here to preach, to get us to turn from our wicked ways? And now you sit here, just hoping that your predictions of doom and destruction will come to pass. Doesn't it matter to you that the people have changed their ways?

JONAH: Not in the least.

NINEVITE: I see. Well, I don't agree with you. I think the Lord God will recognize our repentance and save the city. If not, we might just as well have gone on the way we were.

JONAH: Don't move around so much. You're stirring up the dust. It's all I can do to survive this stifling heat. Why don't you do me a favor and leave me alone?

NINEVITE: Okay, I'll go. Can't say you've been a barrel of laughs, exactly. You know, you'd look a lot better if you'd smile sometimes. Come on, how about a little farewell grin.

JONAH: *(growling)* Go on, get out of here.

(Exit Ninevite. Enter stage manager carrying a paper plant.)

STAGE MANAGER: Now if we had a curtain up here, we'd lower it so we could have an intermission. Of course, in a way it's better that we don't have an intermission, because some of you might not come back, and we haven't passed the collection plate yet. So just be patient and I'll soon have this prop set up. *(Tries setting up paper plant in various positions so as to provide "shade" for Jonah.)* In case you're wondering what this is ... It's a plant, a castor oil plant to be exact, according to the Bible. It says there that the Lord God arranged for a castor oil plant to grow up over Jonah to give shade for his head and soothe his ill humor. Judging from the last scene, I'd say Jonah needs something to brighten up his personality. There, that should do it. *(Exit stage manager)*

JONAH: *(Brightens a bit, sits up, and looks more at ease)* Say, that is better. What a relief not to have that sun beating down on me.

(Enter stage manager)

STAGE MANAGER: But, says the Bible, at dawn the next day, God arranged that a worm should attack the castor oil plant. And it withered. *(Lays paper plant on the floor. Exit stage manager)*

JONAH: *(Expression reverts to one of anger)*
Now what was the point of that? I tell you, this prophet business is for the birds. I get the feeling the Lord God isn't very appreciative of my efforts. I come all the way from Jerusalem to this heathen city, go from one end of it to the other, preaching my heart out, and now it looks as though the Lord is going to relent and spare these miserable people. There's only one day left till the 40 day limit is up, and not a thing to indicate that the city is to be destroyed. And here the sun is, beating down on my poor head. What's the use? I might as well be dead.

(Enter Ninevite)

NINEVITE: *(cheerfully)* Hello there, prophet. *(no response)* Well, I see you're just as cheerful as ever. I thought maybe you'd like to hear about what's going in the city on this last day of the 40 day limit. It might brighten you a bit. The king has declared this a day of prayer and repentance. No one is working today. We've all been urged to stay at home or go to the temples for prayer. Then, tomorrow will be another holiday, a riotous carnival of joy and celebration for our deliverance. How does that strike you, old man?

JONAH:

You seem mighty sure that you'll still be around to celebrate tomorrow.

NINEVITE:

Well, I'm not positive, of course. But every indication is that Nineveh will be spared.

JONAH:

(quietly) You're probably right.

NINEVITE:

(surprised) What did you say?

JONAH:

I said you're probably right. That's the whole trouble with this job. The truth is the Lord doesn't handle this kind of thing the way I would. The Lord is a God of tenderness and compassion, slow to anger, rich in mercy, and abounding in steadfast love.

NINEVITE:

That's bad?

JONAH:

Well, let's just say it's not my idea of the way a God ought to operate.

NINEVITE:

You prefer the fire and brimstone approach.

JONAH:

All I say is that it strikes me as mighty queer that the Lord has more sympathy for a heathen city than for me.

NINEVITE:

You see yourself as a pretty important fellow.

JONAH:

Well ... not all that important. But after all, I am one of the chosen people. I'm one of Abraham's descendants. We received the Divine Law on tablets of stone. We inhabit the holy city of Zion. So the least the Lord could do is to show some concern for me and make my wait comfortable. There was a plant growing here that kept the sun off my head. But apparently I'm not even to have that much enjoyment. There it lies, withered away.

NINEVITE: I see. Well, maybe you do have a legitimate gripe. Seems to be though—if you don't mind my saying so—that you're just making things worse by sitting here feeling sorry for yourself. I mean, maybe you'd feel better if you accepted the way things have turned out. I tell you what ... why don't you come with me back to town? There are some really nice people in Nineveh, yes, even in a "heathen city" like ours, as you put it. And tomorrow ... well, we're going to have a great time. It wouldn't surprise me if they held a special ceremony in your honor. After all, without your warning, we never would have changed our ways and would probably have been destroyed. How about it? Are you coming with me?

JONAH: Don't be ridiculous.

NINEVITE: Okay, have it your way then. *(Pause, begins moving to exit, then turns)* You know, you've been pretty critical of the Lord God. You think the Lord ought to handle things differently and all that. Well, what do you suppose the Lord thinks of you?

JONAH: What do you mean?

NINEVITE: I mean, maybe the Lord's not all that crazy about your performance. Granted, you did your job and got the message across to the people of Nineveh. But what about now ... how do you suppose the Lord feels about your sitting here pouting?

JONAH: I'm not pouting. I'm just looking for some justice. I've lived up to my end of the bargain. What about the Lord's end? As long as the Lord knows I'm still sitting here it will be obvious to the Almighty that

I'm not happy Nineveh hasn't been destroyed.

NINEVITE: In other words, you're hoping to manipulate the Lord into doing what you would like to have done.

JONAH: Well, I wouldn't say ...

NINEVITE: You hope by putting on this sad act that God will feel sorry for you and change things to suit you. "Passive-aggressive," as our psychologists would put it. Well now, what kind of God would constantly give in to people's whims? Not much of one, right, Jonah?

JONAH: Well, maybe not. I don't ...

NINEVITE: *(Turns his/her back to Jonah and speaks in a loud voice)* Jonah, your self pity is an abomination to me. You are angered over this dead plant, which cost you no labor, which you did not make grow, which sprouted in a night and perished in a night. Am I not to have pity on Nineveh, this great city, in which there are more than a hundred and twenty thousand of my children? Go home, Jonah, and cease your complaints. *(Exit Ninevite)*

JONAH: *(utterly amazed)* What the ... *(Gets up and scrambles to follow Ninevite)* Hey, wait ... Who are you? *(Exit Jonah)*

(Enter stage manager)

STAGE MANAGER: *(Collects props as he/she talks)* Well, how about that for a surprise ending? And that's just the way the book of Jonah ends in the Bible. You can look it up yourself. There's no mention of what happened to good old Jonah afterwards. My guess is he went back to Jerusalem a wiser man. And my guess is too, that he never took another sea voyage in his life. *(Exit Stage Manager with props)*

The Millionaires

Adapted from a story by Max Adeler

PRODUCTION NOTES

The mood of "The Millionaires" is subdued and unhurried, in keeping with the time setting of the early 1900s. George and Mary Jane should be seated in rocking chairs with a small table between them containing pencils, a paper tablet, knitting supplies, and a pitcher of water or lemonade. The narrator should be seated at either end of the stage on a high stool. The narrator's speaking style should be conversational and relaxed in the manner of a small town storyteller. Mary Jane can occupy her hands with knitting, while George will frequently be busy with paper and pencil, becoming more agitated with his actions as the play progresses. From time to time, George will get up from his chair to pace worriedly. Mary Jane should remain seated throughout.

Costuming and hair styles should suggest the early part of the twentieth century. Suspenders for George and a long dress for Mary Jane are a must. The narrator can be dressed in either period or contemporary clothing.

This chancel drama was originally performed as reader's theater, with the characters in costume reading their parts rather than having them memorized.

Suggested scripture text: Luke 12:13-21

CAST

George

Mary Jane

Narrator

NARRATOR: It had always been one of the luxuries of the Grimeses to consider what they would do if they were rich. Many a time George and his wife Mary Jane, sitting together of a summer evening upon the porch of their own pretty house in Susanville, had looked at the long unoccupied country estate of General Jenkins, just across the way, and wished they had money enough to buy the place and give it to the village for a park.

Mrs. Grimes often said that if she had a million dollars, the very first thing she would do would be to purchase the Jenkins' place. George's idea was to tear down the fence, throwing everything open, and to dedicate the grounds to the public. Mrs. Grimes wanted to put a great free library in the house and to have a club for poor working women in the second floor rooms. George estimated that one hundred thousand dollars would be enough to carry out their plans. Say fifty thousand dollars for purchase money, and then fifty more invested at six percent, to maintain the place.

GEORGE: But if we had a million, I think I should give one hundred and fifty thousand to the enterprise and do the thing right. There would always be repairs and new books to buy and matters of that kind.

NARRATOR: But this was not the only benevolent dream of these kind-hearted people. They liked to think of the joy that would fill the heart of that poor struggling pastor, Mr. Borrow, if they could tell him that they would pay the whole debt of the Presbyterian Church, six thousand dollars.

MARY JANE: And I would have his salary increased, George. It is shameful to compel that poor man to live on a thousand dollars.

GEORGE:	Outrageous. I would guarantee him another thousand, and maybe more, but we should have to do it quietly, for fear of wounding him.
MARY JANE:	That mortgage on the Methodist Church. Imagine the happiness of those poor people in having it lifted! And so easy to do, too, if we had a million dollars.
GEORGE:	Certainly, and I would give the Baptists a handsome pipe organ instead of that wheezing melodeon. Dreadful, isn't it?
MARY JANE:	You can get a fine organ for two thousand dollars.
GEORGE:	Yes, of course, but I wouldn't be mean about it; not mean on a million dollars. Let them have a really good organ, say for three thousand to three thousand, five hundred; and then build them a parsonage too.
MARY JANE:	The fact is that people like us really ought to have large wealth, for we know how to use it rightly.
GEORGE:	I often think of that. If I know my own soul I long to do good. It makes my heart bleed to see the misery about us, misery we are absolutely unable to relieve. I am sure that if we really had a million dollars we should not want to squander it on mere selfish pleasures. The greatest happiness anyone can have is in making others happy; and it is a wonder to me that our rich people don't see this. Think of old General Jenkins and his twenty million dollars, and what we would do for our neighbors with a mere fraction of that!
MARY JANE:	We really want nothing much for ourselves. We are entirely satisfied with what we have in this lovely little home and with your $2,000 salary from the bank.

GEORGE:	Almost entirely. There are some few little things we might add in, just a few; but with a million we could easily get them and more and have such enormous amounts of money left.
MARY JANE:	Almost the first thing I would do would be to provide a comfortable income for life for poor Isaac Wickersham. That man, George, crippled as he is, lives on next to nothing. I don't believe he has two hundred dollars a year.
GEORGE:	Well, we could give him twelve hundred and not miss it and then give the same sum to Widow Clausen. She can hardly keep alive.
MARY JANE:	And there's another thing I'd do. If we kept a carriage I would never ride up alone from the station or for pleasure, I would always find some poor or infirm person to go with me. How people can be so mean about their horses and carriages as some rich people are is beyond my comprehension.
NARRATOR:	It is a delightful pastime, expending in imagination large sums of money that you haven't got. You need not regard considerations of prudence. You can give free rein to your feelings and bestow your bounty with reckless profusion. You obtain almost all the pleasure of generous giving without any cost. You feel nearly as happy as if you were actually doing the good deeds which are the children of your fancy.
	The pair had considered so often the benevolences they would like to undertake if they had a million dollars that they could have named them all at a moment's notice without referring to a memorandum. Nearly everybody has engaged in this

pastime, but the Grimeses were to have the singular experience of the power to make their dream a reality placed in their hands. For one day, George came flying home from the bank with a letter from the executors of General Jenkins (who had died suddenly in Mexico a week or two before), announcing that the General had left a million dollars and the country estate in Susanville to George Grimes. When the first delirium of their joy had passed, George said:

GEORGE: And to think, Mary Jane, the dear old man was kind enough to say, here, let me read to you again the quotation from the will in the letter: "I make this bequest because, from repeated conversations with the said George Grimes, I know that he will use it aright." So you see, dear, it was worthwhile, wasn't it, to express our benevolent wishes sometimes when we spoke of the needs of those who are around us?

MARY JANE: Yes, and the General's kind remark makes this a sacred trust, which we are to administer for him.

GEORGE: We are only his stewards.

MARY JANE: Stewards for his bounty.

GEORGE: So we must try to do exactly what we think he would have liked us to do.

MARY JANE: Nothing else, dear?

GEORGE: Why, of course we are to have some discretion, some margin; and besides, nobody possibly could guess precisely what he would have us do.

MARY JANE: Not now, at any rate, George, we can realize fully one of our long desires and give to the people the lovely park and library?

GEORGE:
I think, Mary Jane, I would not be too hasty about that. Let us reflect on the matter. It might seem unkind to the memory of the General to give away his gift almost before we get it.

MARY JANE:
Of course there is no hurry. And we are really a little cramped in this house. The nursery is much too small for the children and there is not a decent fruit tree in our garden.

GEORGE:
The thing can just stay open until we have time to consider.

MARY JANE:
But I am so glad for dear old Isaac. We can take care of him, anyhow, and of Mrs. Clausen too.

GEORGE:
To be sure. The obligation is sacred. Let me see, how much was it we thought Isaac ought to have?

MARY JANE:
Twelve hundred a year.

GEORGE:
Hmm. And he has two hundred now; an increase of five hundred percent. I'm afraid it will turn the old man's head. However, I would not exactly promise anything for a few days yet.

MARY JANE:
Many a man in his station in life is happy upon a thousand.

GEORGE:
A thousand! Why, my dear, there is not a man of his class in town that makes six hundred.

MARY JANE:
George?

GEORGE:
Well?

MARY JANE:
We must keep horses, and there is no room to build a stable on this place.

GEORGE:
No.

MARY JANE:	Could we live here and keep the horses in the General's stables across the way, even if the place were turned into a park?
GEORGE:	That is worth thinking of.
MARY JANE:	And George?
GEORGE:	Well, dear?
MARY JANE:	It's a horrid thing to confess, but do you know, George, I've felt myself getting meaner and meaner, and stingier and stingier ever since you brought the good news.
NARRATOR:	George tried to smile, but the effort was unsuccessful; he looked half-vexed and half-ashamed.
GEORGE:	Oh, I wouldn't put it just that way. The news is so exciting that we hardly know at once how to adjust ourselves to it. We are simply prudent. It would be foolish to plunge ahead without any caution at all. How much did you say the debt of the Presbyterian Church is?
MARY JANE:	Six thousand, I think.
GEORGE:	A good deal for a little church like that to owe.
MARY JANE:	Yes, but ...
GEORGE:	You didn't promise anything, Mary Jane, did you, to Mrs. Borrow?
MARY JANE:	No, for I had nothing to promise, but I did tell her on Sunday that I would help them liberally if I could.
GEORGE:	They will base large expectations on that, for sure. I wish you hadn't said it just that way. Of course, we are bound to help them, but I should like to have a perfectly free hand in doing it.

NARRATOR:	There was silence for a moment, while both looked through the window at the General's place over the way.
MARY JANE:	Beautiful, isn't it?
GEORGE:	Lovely. That little annex on the side would make a snug den for me; and imagine the view from that south bedroom window! You would enjoy every look at it.
MARY JANE:	George?
GEORGE:	What?
MARY JANE:	George, dear, tell me frankly, do you really feel in your heart as generous as you did yesterday?
GEORGE:	Now, my dear, why press that matter? Call it meaner or narrower or what you will; maybe I am a little more so than I was; but there is nothing to be ashamed of. It is the conservative instinct asserting itself; the very same faculty in humans that holds society together. I will be liberal enough when the time comes, never fear. I am not going to disregard what one may call the pledges of a lifetime. We will treat everybody right, the Presbyterian Church and Mr. Borrow included. His salary is a thousand, I think you said?
MARY JANE:	Yes.
GEORGE:	Well, I am willing to make it fifteen hundred right now, if you are.
MARY JANE:	We said, you remember, it ought to be two thousand.
GEORGE:	Who said so?
MARY JANE:	You did, on the porch here the other evening.
GEORGE:	I never said so. There isn't a preacher around here gets that much. The Episcopa-

lians with their rich people only give eighteen hundred.

MARY JANE: And a house.

GEORGE: Very well, the Presbyterians can build a house if they want to.

MARY JANE: You consent then to pledge five hundred more to the minister's salary?

GEORGE: I said I would if you would, but my advice is just to let the matter go over until tomorrow or next day, when the whole thing can be considered.

MARY JANE: Very well, but George, sixty thousand dollars is a great deal of money. Sixty thousand in one year we'll get from the interest on the General's bequest. We certainly can afford to be liberal with it, for the General's sake as well as for our own.

GEORGE: Everything depends upon how you look at it. In one way the sum is large. In another way it isn't. General Jenkins had twenty times sixty thousand. Tremendous, isn't it? He might just as well have left us another million. He is in heaven and wouldn't miss it. Then we could have some of our plans more fully carried out.

MARY JANE: I hate to be thought covetous, but I do wish he had put on that other million.

NARRATOR: The next day Mr. Grimes, while sitting with his wife after supper, took a memorandum from his pocket.

GEORGE: I've been jotting down some figures, Mary Jane, just to see how we will come out with our income of sixty thousand dollars.

MARY JANE: Well?

GEORGE: If we give the place across the street for a park and a library and a hundred thousand dollars with which to run it, we shall have just nine hundred thousand left.

MARY JANE: Yes.

GEORGE: We shall want horses, say a carriage pair, and a horse for the wagon. Then I must have a saddle horse and there must be a pony for the children. I thought also you might as well have a gentle pair for your own driving. That makes six. Then there will have to be, say, three stable men. Now, my notion is that we shall put up a larger house further up town with all the necessary stabling. Count the cost of the house and the suitable appointments, and add in the four months' trip to Europe which we decided yesterday to take next summer, and how much of that fifty-four thousand do you think we shall have left at the end of the year?

MARY JANE: But why build the house from our income?

GEORGE: Mary Jane, I want to start out with the fixed idea that we will not cut into our principal.

MARY JANE: Well, how much will we have left?

GEORGE: Not a dollar! The outlay for the year will approximate fifty-six thousand dollars.

MARY JANE: Large, isn't it?

GEORGE: And yet I don't see how we can reduce it if we are to live as people in our circumstances might reasonably be expected to live.

MARY JANE: We must cut off something.

GEORGE: That is what I think. If we give the park and the library building to the town why not let the town pay the cost of caring for them?

MARY JANE:	Then we could save the interest on that other hundred thousand.
GEORGE:	Exactly. And nobody will suffer. The gift of the property alone is magnificent. Who is going to complain of us? We will decide to give the real estate and then stop.
NARRATOR:	Two days later Mr. Grimes came home early from the bank with a letter in his hand. He looked white and for a moment after entering his wife's room, he could hardly speak.
GEORGE:	I have some bad news for you, dear ... terrible news.
NARRATOR:	The thought flashed through Mrs. Grimes' mind that the General had made a later will which had been found and which revoked the bequest to George. She could hardly whisper:
MARY JANE:	What is it?
GEORGE:	The executors write to me that the million dollars left to me by the General draws only four percent interest.
MARY JANE:	George!
GEORGE:	Four percent! Forty thousand dollars instead of sixty thousand! What a frightful loss! Twenty thousand gone at one breath!
MARY JANE:	Are you sure, George?
GEORGE:	Sure? Here is the letter. Read it yourself. One-third of our fortune swept away before we have a chance to touch it!
MARY JANE:	I think it was very unkind of the General to turn the four percents over to us while somebody else gets the six percents. How could he do such a thing? And you such an old friend too!
GEORGE:	Mary Jane, that man always had a mean streak in him. I've said so myself many a

time. But, anyhow, this frightful loss settles one thing; we can't afford to give that property across the street to the town. We must move over there to live, and even then, with the huge expense of keeping such a place in order, we shall have to watch things closely to make ends meet.

MARY JANE: And you never were good at retrenching, George.

GEORGE: But we've got to retrench. Every superfluous expenditure must be cut off. As for the park and free library, that seems wild now, doesn't it? I don't regret abandoning the scheme. The people of this town never did appreciate public spirit or generosity, did they?

MARY JANE: Never.

GEORGE: I'm very sorry you spoke to Mrs. Borrow about helping their church. Do you think she remembers it?

MARY JANE: She met me today and said they were expecting something handsome.

GEORGE: That's always the way with those people. They are the worst beggars! When a lot of folks get together and start a church, it is almost indecent for them to come running around to ask other folks to support it. I have half a notion not to give them a cent.

MARY JANE: Not even for Mr. Borrow's salary?

GEORGE: Certainly not! Half the clergymen in the United States get less than a thousand dollars a year; why can't he do as the rest do? Am I to be called upon to support a lot of poor preachers? A good deal of nerve it takes to ask such a thing of me.

NARRATOR: Two weeks afterwards, Mr. and Mrs. Grimes sat together again on the porch in the cool of the evening.

GEORGE: Now. Let's go over these charities we were talking about and be done with them. Let's start with the hard fact staring us in the face that, with only one million dollars at four percent, and all our new and necessary expenses, we shall have to look sharp or I'll be borrowing money to live on in less than eight months.

MARY JANE: Well, what should we cut out? Would you give up the Baptist organ that we used to talk about?

GEORGE: Mary Jane, it is really surprising how you let such things as that stay in your mind. I considered that organ idea abandoned long ago.

MARY JANE: Is it worthwhile, do you think, to do anything with the Methodist Church mortgage?

GEORGE: How much is it?

MARY JANE: Three thousand dollars, I think.

GEORGE: Yes, three thousand from forty thousand leaves only thirty-seven thousand. Then, if we do it for the Methodists we shall have to do it for the Lutherans and the Presbyterians and swarms of churches all around the country. We can't make flesh of one and fowl of another. It will be safer to treat them all alike; and more just too. I think we ought to try to be just with them, don't you, Mary Jane?

MARY JANE: And Mr. Borrow's salary?

GEORGE: Ha! Yes! That is a thousand dollars, isn't it? It does seem but a trifle. But they have no children and they have themselves completely adjusted to it. And suppose we would raise it one year and die the next? He would feel worse than if he just went along in the old way. When a man is fully adjusted to a thing, it is the part of prudence, it seems to me, just to let him alone.

MARY JANE: I wish we could ...

GEORGE: Oh well, if you want to; but I propose we don't make them the offer until next year or the year after. We shall have our matters arranged better by that time.

MARY JANE: And how about Isaac Wickersham?

GEORGE: Have you seen him lately?

MARY JANE: Two or three days ago.

GEORGE: Did he seem discontented or unhappy?

MARY JANE: No.

GEORGE: You promised to help him?

MARY JANE: What I said was, "We are going to do something for you, Isaac."

GEORGE: Something! That commits us to nothing in particular. Was it your idea, Mary Jane, to make an allowance?

MARY JANE: Yes.

GEORGE: There! You cut into our insufficient income again. I don't see how we can afford it with all these expenses heaping up on us. I really don't.

MARY JANE: But George, I did promise ...

GEORGE: All right. This is the end of September and I won't need that straw hat I've been wearing all summer. Suppose you give him that. A good straw hat is "something."

MARY JANE: You remember Mrs. Clausen, George?

GEORGE: Must we throw away something on her too?

MARY JANE: Let me explain. You recall that I told her I would try to make her comfortable, and when I found out that our circumstances were going to be really ... uh ... tight. I sent her my red flannel petticoat with my love, for I know she can be comfortable in that.

So this afternoon when I came up from the city she got out of the train with me and I felt so half-ashamed of the gift that I pretended not to see her and hurried out to the carriage and drove quickly up the hill. She is afraid of horses anyhow.

GEORGE: Always was.

MARY JANE: But, George, I don't feel quite right about it yet; the gift of a petticoat is rather stingy, isn't it?

GEORGE: No, I don't think so.

MARY JANE: And, George, to be perfectly honest with ourselves now, don't you think we are a little bit meaner than we were, say, last June?

NARRATOR: George cleared his throat and hesitated, and then he said:

GEORGE: I admit nothing, excepting that the only people who are fit to have money are the people who know how to take care of it.

Lazarus Unbound

PRODUCTION NOTES

The story of Lazarus being raised from the dead is one of the most poignant and dramatic in the Bible. Living as we do in what some people call the "post-Christian era," we have trouble dealing with the raising of Lazarus. We ask questions of it that likely would not have occurred to early Christian believers. In this play, some of those questions get asked by Lazarus himself. Other questions are raised by his interrogator, Mark Callis. The setting for the play is a contemporary TV interview program. Lazarus should be depicted as a thoroughly modern character. Accordingly, he should be dressed in contemporary clothing, as should Callis. The action of the play occurs shortly after Jesus raised Lazarus from the dead. However, the play imaginatively places this event in the present. The set consists simply of two comfortable chairs partly facing each other and partly facing the audience.

Suggested scripture text: John 11:1-44

CAST

LAZARUS

MARK CALLIS
interviewer

(Callis and Lazarus enter. Callis is attaching microphone at his neck as they sit down, then leans over to assist Lazarus adjust his mike.)

CALLIS: *(Loudly)* Okay, guys, we all set up? *(To Lazarus in conversational tone)* Now all you gotta do is talk natural. This thing'll pick up everything. And, uh, don't bother about looking at the cameras. Act like it's just the two of us here having a chat. Okay?

LAZARUS: I guess so.

CALLIS: Okay, 15 seconds to go. Freddy, don't forget to keep the sound level up ... not like the last time. Okay? Give me the cue. *(Assumes "TV voice")* Good evening. Welcome to "A Closer Look." I'm your host, Mark Callis. The subject of our interview this week is one Lazarus, resident of the small village of Bethany and celebrity of sorts since an event which purportedly took place two weeks ago. *(To Lazarus)* Good evening, Mr. Lazarus. Tell us, in your own words, what exactly happened to you?

LAZARUS: I was raised from the dead.

CALLIS: You were "raised from the dead"?

LAZARUS: That's right.

CALLIS: I see. Now, just so there can be no mistake ... you weren't in a coma, or some deep sleep. You were actually dead.

LAZARUS: Yes, dead and buried.

CALLIS: The news accounts said that you were dead for four days before this, ah, "resurrection" took place. Is that correct?

LAZARUS: Yes, it is.

CALLIS: We have statements here from a rabbi, a physician, and your two sisters, all establishing that you were pronounced dead, and given a customary burial. So it would appear that you really were dead, Mr. Lazarus.

LAZARUS: Yes, it would.

CALLIS: Before we explore this unusual event in a bit more depth, why don't you tell us a little bit about yourself. Where you were born, what you do for a living, that kind of thing.

LAZARUS: Well, there's not really much to tell. I was born and raised right here in Bethany. My folks were humble people, devout in their religious practice. My father insisted that I take my studies with the rabbis seriously.

CALLIS: Your parents are both dead, is that right?

LAZARUS: Yes, they both died some years ago.

CALLIS: And you and your sisters have remained living here. Their names are Mary and Martha, I believe.

LAZARUS: Yes.

CALLIS: Uh huh. Anything more you'd like to add?

LAZARUS: Not much really. I took over my father's small carpentry business when he died. I make a decent living, enough to provide for myself and my sisters.

CALLIS: Carpentry. Tell me, isn't or wasn't that the trade of Jesus of Nazareth before he turned into a ... teacher ... and a ...healer?

LAZARUS: That's right.

CALLIS: Well, of course, a big part of this whole story has to do with this Jesus. Stories have been floating around for some time now about miracles he's performed up north, healing lepers, casting out demons. One story even has it that he brought back to life a little girl who had died. But that's the kind of thing we're used to hearing from Galilee. The people up there are, as I'm sure you'll agree, mostly uneducated and superstitious. But now Jesus comes to Jerusalem itself and apparently pulls off a spectacular revivification just a few miles from the city. Tell us something about this Jesus, Mr. Lazarus. How did you meet him?

LAZARUS: My sister Martha is the devout one in our family. She never misses Sabbath worship. Anyway, this one time she heard about a rabbi from Nazareth who had come to town. Now, there are two things you should know about my sister. First, she has what is almost a worship for any rabbi (just as our parents did), and secondly, she has the reputation as the best cook in Bethany. So naturally, Jesus wound up as our dinner guest.

CALLIS: And that's when you met him?

LAZARUS: Yes. We'd had lots of similar guests before, as I said, Martha is a fantastic cook, so at first I didn't pay much attention to him. But then I heard him talking with Mary. She's my younger sister. A lot like me. She doesn't put much stock in the religion of our parents. She's a skeptic, loves to heckle the rabbis that Martha drags home for a free meal. I generally ignore them altogether. They're a dreadfully stuffy lot, if you want my opinion.

CALLIS: From what I've heard of him, the word "stuffy" would not apply to Jesus.

LAZARUS: Right! When I overheard this Jesus talking to Mary, I noticed right away something different about him. I mean, usually she needles them to death. They start stammering and sputtering. Then she tells them she doesn't believe in God at all, that Abraham and Moses were misguided fools. *(laughs)*

Oh, that woman has a wicked tongue, let me tell you. Of course, she does it all for fun, but they don't take it that way. And then Martha comes to the rescue with one of her delicious soup appetizers, and the rabbis lose all interest in religious debate. Which only goes to prove, as Mary says, that the most religious part of any man is his stomach. *(laughs)* Half the time, our distinguished guests are so ravenous for Martha's soups that they must be reminded to lay down their spoons and say the blessing.

CALLIS: But about Jesus, Mr. Lazarus.

LAZARUS: Oh yes. Well, like I said, it was different with him. Mary wasn't giving him any guff. Her questions were serious ones. And he answered them with understanding and even intelligence. So I joined them. Now don't get me wrong. Some of what he said seemed pretty far out to me. But the thing about him that struck me was his ... his sincerity. No, that's not the right word. Transparency ... maybe that's it. I mean, he didn't seem to have up the false front, the mask, that nearly all of us wear. He wasn't playing a role. He was just himself. And that's the way he treated us too. Like we were somebody.

CALLIS: And so that's how you became one of his disciples?

LAZARUS: Disciple? Not on your life! I'm not his disciple. I've got too much self-respect to be any man's disciple.

CALLIS: Then what was your relationship to him?

LAZARUS: I don't know. I ... I ... never really thought about it.

CALLIS:	But there must have been some kind of relationship. Why else would he raise you from the dead?
LAZARUS:	Yes. I've wondered that myself. I don't ... I don't ... know.
CALLIS:	Was he your friend?
LAZARUS:	*(dazed)* Yes ... I suppose he was. Yes ... he was ... is ... my friend.
CALLIS:	Frankly, Mr. Lazarus, I'm having real trouble putting this whole thing together. Do you know what rumors are now flying about your "friend" as you put it?
LAZARUS:	*(still in a daze)* No. I don't know.
CALLIS:	*(tone hardens)* Well, the word is that this self-appointed rabbi has some high ambitions. That he's out to discredit the whole religious establishment and wants to win enough popular support to get himself appointed high priest. They say he's using his "miracles" as a means to this end, that he claims special divine guidance for all he does, and that any day now, probably around Passover time, he's going to lead his supporters to a confrontation in Jerusalem with the powers that be.
LAZARUS:	I don't pay much attention to political gossip.
CALLIS:	Maybe you haven't heard what they're saying about you.
LAZARUS:	*(shows a bit more interest)* No. *(mockingly)* What are "they" saying about me?
CALLIS:	Hmm. Seems you are interested in some political gossip. Well, "they" are saying, Mr. Lazarus, that you're in cahoots with him, that you've known him for a lot longer than you let on. "They" say that you're his agent, living here just outside

Jerusalem, keeping a weather eye on the political climate, passing the word back to him. You've been in it with him all the way!

LAZARUS: *(calmly and with a smile)* Your sources have been badly misinformed, Mr. Callis.

CALLIS: Oh really! Then I'm sure you won't mind explaining a few things for our viewers. Like, for example, didn't Jesus, while visiting in your home, make unfavorable references to certain religious parties?

LAZARUS: I don't remember. I told you, politics doesn't interest me.

CALLIS: *(sarcastically)* Of course, Mr. Lazarus. I forgot. Politics doesn't interest you. What about religion? Does that interest you? You tell us that you never attend the synagogue, that you have nothing but contempt for the rabbis that come for Martha's chicken dinners. Now along comes this carpenter's son. You listen to him for one afternoon and suddenly you're his "friend." It can't be his political views that lead to friendship; you're not "interested" in politics. And it can't be his religious views that make you his friend, because you despise religion. Exactly what was it that inspired this "friendship"?

LAZARUS: *(defensively, but quietly)* I told you it was not what he said so much as his ... his manner, his way of speaking.

CALLIS: Come now, Mr. Lazarus, do you really expect us to believe that? Out of one afternoon grows a friendship so powerful that it compels Jesus to come out of hiding in the desert where he had fled to regroup his forces, to journey several days into enemy territory here at Jerusalem's front door, all on a mere report that you were sick? Can you blame us if we're a bit suspicious when you tell us that this grand friendship was based, not on any points of agreement between you, but solely on "his way of speaking"?

LAZARUS: *(calmly)* Whether you or anyone else believes it is of no concern of mine.

CALLIS: *(sharply)* Do you deny that threats have recently been made on your life?

LAZARUS: I will not deny it. Neither will I confirm it.

CALLIS: Word is that the high priest's henchmen plan to give you a second chance at this dying business. Only this time your tomb will be at the bottom of the river.

LAZARUS: I see.

CALLIS: *(explodes)* Come off it, Lazarus. You're not fooling anyone with this "I-couldn't-care-less" attitude. You're scared; admit it! The whole story is out. This resurrection bit was a phony from start to finish. It was his trump card, a bid to make everybody believe he was God's appointed kingpin, his right-hand man. The plan is to have you get suddenly sick, die, and then Jesus comes galloping to the rescue. He'll go to the grave, say a few hocus-pocus words, and out you come, looking bright-eyed and bushy-tailed. Only something went wrong, didn't it, Lazarus? Jesus decides he wants to make it look really good. So when he gets the "message" that you're sick, he delays things a few days. Why? Any real friend would have been here right away. But he stays put for two whole days! And then he tells his followers, now where is it? We got a quote from one of them. I want to get this exactly right. Here it is: "He said to us, Lazarus is dead; and for your sake I am glad that I was not there, so that you may believe." That's some friendship you got there, Lazarus! No sir, the reason he took his good old time was that he knew you weren't dead at all. It was all a set-up. So when he finally gets here, it will look as though you've been dead four whole days. Enough to convince even the most recalcitrant doubter. The only thing he didn't figure on was that you might get a little woozy wrapped up in all those bandages. The fact is you almost did pack it in by the time he showed up. Wouldn't that have been a spectacle? He comes bouncing up to the tomb, calls out, "Lazarus, come forth!" and nothing happens. And there would have gone his whole campaign, buried under the laughter and ridicule of friends and enemies alike. But you hung on, didn't you, Lazarus? I can't imagine what you were thinking, sealed up in that tomb, waiting for him to show. Did you think he'd betrayed you, forgotten you? Tell us, Lazarus. What went through your mind? Did you "get religion" towards the end? *(shouting)* Tell us, Lazarus. Tell everyone! *(pause) (Abrupt change of mood. Stands and takes off his mike)* Okay, that's it. Cut! Stop the cameras. It's no use. The interview's off. This has been about as thrilling a piece of journalism as a knitting demonstration. I said that's it, Lazarus. It's off. Kaput. You savvy, great stone face? But tell me something. What was in it for you? What was the pay-off? Did he promise wealth? Women? Little boys?

LAZARUS: *(finally explodes)* All right, you two-bit hack! Out! Get out of my sight! And take your playthings with you. *(Stands and tears off microphone)* You've had your interview; now beat it!

CALLIS: Oh no. Ohh no. Huh uh. Not till I get to the bottom of this. Maybe the interview's over. But I'm going to stick around till I find out what makes you tick.

LAZARUS: *(Sinks wearily into chair and covers face in hands)* Please go away. I just want to rest.

CALLIS: Is that why you agreed to this interview, to have it all over and done with?

LAZARUS: *(Pause) (Takes hands away from face. Looks at Callis and smiles ruefully)*
You know something? Your version of the whole thing sounds more believable than the way it really was.

CALLIS: *(sits)* How was it ... really?

LAZARUS: Your trouble, Callis, is that you believe a big story is the best thing life has to offer. I pity you. That's such a puny thing to sell your soul for.

CALLIS: *(Soberly and uneasily)* Maybe you're right. What is worth selling one's soul for? Your soul, for instance.

LAZARUS: My soul. I've begun to wonder if I have a soul. And yet I must. The rabbis say every man has a soul. I am a man. Therefore, by the rational process of deductive reasoning, I have a soul.

CALLIS: Why are you so unhappy? I should think a man come back from the dead would be happy as a lark.

LAZARUS: *(Looks at Callis sharply)*

CALLIS: No, please. I didn't mean that sarcastically. I ... I think I really meant it. You puzzle me.

LAZARUS: Yes, no doubt I do. Well, I'm puzzled too. But that's not the worst of it. The fact is I'm not sure if something didn't happen to me there in that tomb. I feel like a creature out of my element. No longer at home in this life and yet not quite ready for the next.

CALLIS: *(Laughs sardonically)*

Oh, you don't have to have been resurrected to feel that way!

LAZARUS: Meaning?

CALLIS: Let's just say that the life of a celebrity reporter is not without its depressing moments. *(pause)* They tell me that he wept for you.

LAZARUS: Who? Jesus? Yes, so I've heard.

CALLIS: That is something at least. I mean, of course, if it wasn't all part of the act. But you don't seem much ... moved by it. His weeping for you, I mean.

LAZARUS: Let's get one thing straight. I didn't ask to be raised from the dead! It was all his doing, and what his motives were I have no way of knowing. Mary tells me he did it because he loved me. But then she's in love with him herself. I mean, why ... how could he love me? He doesn't even know me.

CALLIS: I've heard that he has a way of divining what is in people's hearts.

LAZARUS: *(surprised)* Why, my dear journalist friend, I do believe you're on the verge of becoming one of his followers yourself. So that's why you wanted this interview!

CALLIS: *(A bit too hastily)* Don't be ridiculous! I've seen these headline-grabbers come and go for years now. Another month or two and he'll be just another has-been. Only ...

LAZARUS: Only what?

CALLIS: Well, just for the sake of argument, let's suppose he's on the level. All his preaching about abundant life and so on. If he's actually got a message, why doesn't he talk to the really important people, and try to win them to his side? Why waste his time on the poor, the ignorant? Forgive me, on such unknowns as yourself?

LAZARUS: I've asked myself that question and a hundred more like it dozens of times in the past two weeks.

CALLIS: And what have you decided?

LAZARUS: *(Stands and begins to pace)* Nothing! Literally nothing. I just don't know! Why did he risk his neck to come here and bring me out of the tomb? Why didn't he just leave me there ... forever? Then I wouldn't be tormented by these questions.

CALLIS: *(pause)* But then you never would have known that he ... he ... loved you. *(Can't believe what he has just said)* Love! That's another of those empty words. Like truth and faith and ... Once ... once I believed in them. Long ago. There was this ... She and I ... *(catches himself)* Sorry. Almost got carried away there.

LAZARUS: *(Has been listening carefully)*
You know something, Mark. You and I are a lot alike.

CALLIS: How's that?

LAZARUS: On the outside we have this layer of sophistication and skepticism. But inside we're both frightened little boys.

CALLIS: Maybe you're right. I've been thinking about the tomb, Lazarus. You came out of it alive. Quite an accomplishment. But yet not alive. I think we're both in a tomb of our own making. Call it unbelief. Call it self-hatred. Call it despair. We're inside it, still waiting for resurrection.

LAZARUS: Yes. Thank you for that. Maybe ... maybe it doesn't have to be this way.

CALLIS: Who knows? *(stands)* But thank you for helping me see things a bit more clearly.

(Reaches out his hand. Lazarus stands and they exchange a firm handshake)
Well, I've got to be going. Oh. Hey fellows, you can stop the cameras. We're all done.

LAZARUS: You mean ...?

CALLIS: Oh, I'm sorry. That blow-up awhile ago was an old reporter's trick. People talk more freely when they think it's off the record. *(pause)* Funny thing. I forgot all about the camera myself soon afterwards. Doesn't matter. We can't use it. Nobody'd be interested in the soul confessions of two ... ah ... tomb-mates.

LAZARUS: *(laughs)* What a terrible pun. At least you didn't say "the situation looks very grave."

CALLIS: You're right. I didn't. I wouldn't! Anyhow, maybe things aren't quite as grave for us as they were half an hour ago.

LAZARUS: Maybe. Good-bye.

CALLIS: Good-bye.

(They exit in different directions)

A
Story

PRODUCTION NOTES

This little play offers a modest lesson about truth. Junior or senior high youth may assume the roles. As the narrator begins speaking, the other characters take their places on stage and assume positions appropriate to their roles. Costuming needs only to suggest the characters. For example, the tree may hold leaves or small branches; the rose may wear leaves, petals, and even thorns made of construction paper, etc. The actions of each character should fit the part. The ant, for instance, might be busy moving earth in pantomime; the rose might preen and look in a mirror admiringly.

Suggested scripture text: James 3:13-18

CAST

(NARRATOR: *enters, stands at pulpit. Other charac-*
ters assume places on stage, turn their backs to
audience until they are engaged in stage action)

NARRATOR: With a little help from some friends of mine, I'd like to tell you a story. It's a very simple story, and I don't know if it really happened quite this way, but maybe it did. Some of you may think this story is for children. Perhaps it is, but I'm reminded of One who once said: "unless you become as little children . . ." This is a story about a raindrop.

"Now that's silly," you may say. "How could a raindrop be a character in a story?" Nevertheless, this story is about a raindrop. Her/His name? Well, that's not really so important, but if you must know, it was Renée/René. At least, that's what her/his friends called her/him.

Renée/René was a young raindrop, just getting her/his feet wet in life, so to speak. And she/he had a lot of questions. About life and truth and things like that. And so one day she/he asked the wind if it would help her/him do some traveling. The wind, in a pleasant, breezy state of mind that day, agreed to help her/him out.

So it was that our raindrop was carried first of all to a spot where she/he saw someone working busily.

RENÉE/RENÉ: Hello there.

ANT: What?

RENÉE/RENÉ: I said hello. *(pause)* Aren't you going to say hello?

ANT: Nope, don't have time.

RENÉE/RENÉ: You're working very hard. You're an ant, aren't you?

ANT: Yep.

Renée/René:	Why do you work so hard?
Ant:	Questions, questions, questions. You kids are all the same. When I was your age, I didn't have time for questions. I was busy working.
Renée/René:	Do you enjoy your work?
Ant:	It's not a matter of enjoyment. It's something that has to be done.
Renée/René:	Why must it be done?
Ant:	Because it must, that's why. If you don't work in this world, you'll never get ahead. Trouble with kids today is they don't have any ambition. Let me tell you something. You've got to work hard, save your money, plan ahead or else you won't amount to anything.
Renée/René:	I see. What do you do for relaxation?
Ant:	Don't have time. This work must be kept after. I can't afford to waste time. It's too precious. It's later than you think, you know.
Renée/René:	Don't you ever stop to enjoy the beautiful flowers or hear the birds singing?
Ant:	Nope. They're overrated anyway. Take it from me; you've seen one flower you've seen them all. And the singing of the birds? That's for the birds.
Renée/René:	But isn't all this work rather . . . dull? All work and no play, you know.
Ant:	Never thought about it. Say, are you soon finished? I'm a busy ant, you know.
Renée/René:	Yes, I see. Well, thanks. You're the first one I've talked to about what the truth is in life.
Ant:	The truth? That's easy. Hard work and more hard work. That's the ticket. Well,

RENÉE/RENÉ:

NARRATOR:

RENÉE/RENÉ:

FLOWER:

RENÉE/RENÉ:

FLOWER:

RENÉE/RENÉ:

FLOWER:

RENÉE/RENÉ:

FLOWER:

RENÉE/RENÉ:

FLOWER:

RENÉE/RENÉ:

FLOWER:

RENÉE/RENÉ:

FLOWER:

good-bye. Keep your nose to the grindstone.

Good-bye.

And so our raindrop moved on, turning over in her/his mind what the ant had told her/him. Could it be that hard work was the secret of life?

Maybe this creature has a different idea. Hello, you're a flower, aren't you?

Yes, I am.

My name is Renée/René. I'm a raindrop. What's your name?

I can see you're a raindrop. My name is Rose.

"Rose." That's a pretty name. *(sighs)* I think you're beautiful.

Yes, I know.

Rose, maybe you can help me. I'm trying to learn the truth about life. The last creature I talked to said it was hard work. What do you think?

(Not really paying attention) Hmmm?

I said, do you think hard work is the truth about life?

(Suddenly hears the question) Hard work? Of course not!

(eagerly) Then what is the truth?

Why, it's beauty and happiness, getting all the good things you can out of life.

That sounds like fun!

Oh, it is. There's so much misery in life; so I try to forget it. I love to read poetry, sing songs, and let the breeze blow through my lovely petals.

RENÉE/RENÉ:	Aren't you worried about . . . uh . . . "getting ahead"?
FLOWER:	*(laughs)* Don't be silly! I don't worry about anything. In fact, if things start getting me down, I . . . ah . . . *(Leans toward Renée/René and lowers voice)* take a trip.
RENÉE/RENÉ:	Take a trip? How do you do that?
FLOWER:	*(confidentially)* Well, if you know the right creature, you can buy a little blue pill that will take your mind off all your troubles. It's really wonderful.
RENÉE/RENÉ:	So you have friends?
FLOWER:	Well, no, not really. I had a friend once. But friends are always asking you for favors or they get into trouble and want you to help them. I don't like to be involved with unhappiness, so I'd rather be on my own.
RENÉE/RENÉ:	Thank you for your help. You would say that the truth about life is to find happiness.
FLOWER:	That's it. Do your own thing. Enjoy life. Remember, "life is just a bowl of cherries."
NARRATOR:	A second idea about truth. This one appealed more than the first to our little raindrop, but she/he still wasn't satisfied. And so she/he was off again. This time she/he ended up at the foot of a big tree.
RENÉE/RENÉ:	Hello. *(pause)* *(louder)* Hello!
TREE:	Oh, hello down there. You must speak up, I could hardly hear you.
RENÉE/RENÉ:	You certainly are tall and strong. I'll bet you're the biggest creature in the whole forest.
TREE:	Well, I'm one of the biggest, anyhow.

RENÉE/RENÉ:	Someone as strong as you must know a lot about life. What is the truth about life?
TREE:	Well, youngster, let me tell you. Life belongs to the strong, the powerful. Look around you. What creatures do you look up to respect? Why it's the strong ones, that's who. So if you want to know the secret of life, I can tell you in one word: "power."
RENÉE/RENÉ:	The last creature I asked told me it was beauty and happiness.
TREE:	Who was that?
RENÉE/RENÉ:	Her name was Rose, the flower.
TREE:	*(scornfully)* Oh yes, I know her. Come back in a few weeks and she'll have withered away. But someone like me will be around a long time.
RENÉE/RENÉ:	I see. How would I go about becoming powerful like you?
TREE:	Any way you can. You have to look out for yourself. When I was young, lots of bushes and trees would have kept me small and stunted if I had let them. I had to assert myself, play rough when necessary, fight my way to the top, and so here I stand . . . a self-made tree.
RENÉE/RENÉ:	I certainly am impressed. But what enjoyment do you get out of life?
TREE:	I enjoy the competition of staying on top. That's all that counts.
RENÉE/RENÉ:	I see. Thank you for your advice. I must be going now.
TREE:	Well, good luck. And remember: winning isn't everything; it's the only thing.
NARRATOR:	By this time our friend was thoroughly confused. Which creature was right? Truth seemed hard to find. And so, with

her/his head spinning, she/he sat down to rest.

PEBBLE: What makes you so tired?

RENÉE/RENÉ: Oh, hi there. I guess my brain is tired, that's all. I've been trying to find out what the truth is.

PEBBLE: And what have you found?

RENÉE/RENÉ: That everyone has a different idea about it.

PEBBLE: *(laughs)* Yes, you're right. I learned that long ago.

RENÉE/RENÉ: Did you search for truth yourself. You, a little pebble?

PEBBLE: Sure, why not? I wasn't always a little pebble, you know. I started out as part of a big boulder.

RENÉE/RENÉ: How did you get to be a pebble?

PEBBLE: Well, I learned very early that life is best when you put it into the hands of the Maker. So I've been actually been many places and been many things.

RENÉE/RENÉ: Who is this Maker you just mentioned?

PEBBLE: You don't know who the Maker is?

RENÉE/RENÉ: *(Shakes her head)*

PEBBLE: *(kindly)* You are young, aren't you? How did you imagine you came to be in the first place?

RENÉE/RENÉ: *(Slowly, a bit embarrassed)* I guess I never really thought about it.

PEBBLE: I see. Well, the Maker is the One who created all the creatures and created you. The Maker has something for each of us to do, and we are happiest when we are doing what the Maker wants us to do.

RENÉE/RENÉ: You did what the Maker wanted you to do?

PEBBLE: Yes. Once I was part of a stone wall in a beautiful building. Once I was used to support a bridge.

RENÉE/RENÉ: What do you do now?

PEBBLE: Now I lie here, forming part of a road for folks to travel on.

RENÉE/RENÉ: But what about power . . . and beauty... and getting ahead?

PEBBLE: All the power there is comes from the Maker, and any creature who is powerful is so only because the Maker allows it. Getting ahead? Getting ahead of whom? If you think in those terms, you'll always be killing yourself to beat your neighbor. As for happiness . . . well, I've had many friends over the years. That's how my happiness comes, from helping them and being loved by them. I'd like to have you as my friend.

RENÉE/RENÉ: You would? That's wonderful! No other creature said that to me. Thank you! (pause) Tell me, my new friend, how can I do anything for the Maker? I'm so small.

PEBBLE: Yes, but think how you can be used. You can water a plant or wash dirt away or give a drink to a thirsty traveler. There are hundreds of things you can do.

RENÉE/RENÉ: (eagerly) Yes, of course. I'll postpone my search for truth and begin doing whatever the Maker can use me for.

PEBBLE: Little friend, you have no further need to search for truth. You have found it.

Right
Man
for the
Job

PRODUCTION NOTES

The Old Testament concept of God often included the idea of a heavenly council, with the Lord surrounded by beings who did God's bidding. Sometimes these beings were called angels; their task was essentially that of bearing messages. Later on, the idea of angels was personalized by assigning names to them.

In this play, an imaginary conversation takes place between the Lord and an angel. I stress the word "imaginary," because, although most of the exchange between the Lord and Moses is taken from the book of Exodus, there is nothing in the Bible to support the dialogue which occurs between Gabriel and the Lord.

The Lord should wear something to convey authority and set his or her character apart from Gabriel and Moses. A black clerical robe will do nicely. Otherwise, the costumes and props should be in a contemporary mode. In Scene One, the Lord can be seated at a small desk cluttered with papers, pencils, etc.

For Scene Two, the "burning bush" can be suggested by a red spotlight trained on a live or artificial bush. Alternatively, the "bush" can be offstage, with Moses facing in an offstage direction. Keep the play moving. Gabriel's agitated movements about the stage should contrast with the Lord's calm, in-charge demeanor.

Suggested scripture text: Exodus 3:1-12

CAST

THE LORD: This character can be portrayed by either a
male or female. The Lord should be authori-
tative, yet personable.

GABRIEL: A not-too-bright, agitated, but sincere angel.

MOSES: This character need not look anything like
Charlton Heston!

Scene 1

(The Lord is seated at a desk, wearily reading reports and making occasional notations)

GABRIEL: *(Enters, bowing very low)* Most Holy One, God of Gods, Lord of Hosts, Almighty Sovereign, I am your humble servant, Gabriel. You sent for me, and I am come. Amen.

THE LORD: *(Looks up from his/her work distractedly)* Huh? Oh yes, Gabriel. Uh, stand up, stand up. *(Goes back to work while Gabriel stands there uncomfortably)* Well, then, Gabriel, what is it? Speak up, I'm way behind in my paperwork. Yes, paperwork. How did you think I looked after things? Clap my hands? Throw out some lightning bolts? Toss miracles around at will? *(sighs)* Sometimes I wish it were as simple as everyone imagines it to be. But speak up, man! Don't stand there gaping at me! You're here for a reason. What is it?

GABRIEL: Most Holy One, God of Gods, Lord of Hosts, Almighty Sovereign, I am your humble servant, Gabriel. You sent for me and I am come. Amen.

THE LORD: I "sent for you"? Oh, yes. Yes, I did, come to think of it. Now let me see, why did I send for you?

GABRIEL: Most Holy One, God of Gods, Lord of Hosts, Almighty Sovereign ... might it have been about the children of Israel?

THE LORD: The children of Israel! Of course, of course. You're the one we've assigned to keep tabs on them. Yes. In fact, not long ago I was reading one of your reports,

Gabriel. Very disturbing, I must say. Upsetting. I don't like the way things are going. Let's see, where is that report? Here it is, oppression, cruelty, slavery, old men forced to do back-breaking labor, women made old before their time, infants slaughtered ... Very discouraging, Gabriel. Very discouraging. (*reads*) "The people are crying out to God for relief from their oppression." This calls for action, Gabriel. Decisive action. We've got to do something. What do you suggest?

GABRIEL: (*shocked*) M-m-most Holy One, G-g-god of Gods, L-l-lord of...

THE LORD: Now see here, Gabriel. You and I have lots of work to do. If you keep prefacing everything you say with all those titles, we'll waste a lot of valuable time. Suppose you address me as ... uh ... "Lord God" and the rest of it will be more or less understood. All right?

GABRIEL: Y-y-yes, Lord God.

THE LORD: Good. Now, answer my question. What do you suggest we do about this horrible suffering of the Israelites at the hand of Pharaoh?

GABRIEL: But, Lord God ... begging your pardon ... but why do you ask me? I'm just your basic angel. You are the Most Holy One, the God of Gods.

THE LORD: Yes, yes. I know that! I do have a pretty good idea of what I'm going to do. But you've been watching the situation closely for some time now. I'm genuinely interested in what you think ought to be done.

GABRIEL: You mean, what would I do if I were you ... begging your pardon, Lord God, at even suggesting the thought.

THE LORD:	Yes, I suppose that's what I mean, Gabriel. What would you do if you were the Lord God?
GABRIEL:	Lord God, that's hard to answer. I've never even thought in those terms.
THE LORD:	Oh really? Then why is it that I'm continually hearing people say things like: "How could God do such a thing?" and "Why did God permit this to happen to me?" and "If it were up to me, I'd do such and such"? It seems everybody has some pretty strong notions about how they'd run things if they were in my shoes.
GABRIEL:	But, Lord God, I don't believe they really mean it when they say such things. Mostly they are just reacting emotionally to fear or grief or something like that. They don't actually want to be God.
THE LORD:	H-m-m-m. Maybe so, maybe so. Still it is irritating to hear them all implying they could do a much better job than I. But Gabriel, I think you're trying to wiggle your way off the spot. What do you suggest we do in this Israelite situation?
GABRIEL:	Well ... I ... that is ... maybe we could ... no, that won't do. Perhaps ... No ...
THE LORD:	You're not a very decisive fellow, are you Gabriel?
GABRIEL:	I've got it, Lord. How about sending a great flood on the earth, a flood which will drown all the Egyptians, but none of the Israelites?
THE LORD:	How will we keep from drowning the Israelites?
GABRIEL:	We could put them in a big boat.
THE LORD:	(drily) We could call it an ark.
GABRIEL:	Yes. (with uncertainty)

An ark. That sounds familiar.

THE LORD: Gabriel, I tried that method once before. It worked for exactly one generation and then things were as bad as ever. The flood method is out.

GABRIEL: How about an earthquake to destroy everything that moves in Egypt? *(muses to himself)* Nope, that won't work; how would we keep the Israelites safe? *(brightens)* I've got it! How about raising up a great general among the Israelites and have them slaughter all the Egyptians?

THE LORD: The idea of death has a certain fascination for you, Gabriel. A certain appeal. Have you noticed that? I tell you, I've seen too much of fighting and war. It causes too much suffering, and it rarely settles anything. What other ideas do you have?

GABRIEL: Well, as I see it, the Pharaoh is a big part of the problem. If we can straighten him out, our problem is solved.

THE LORD: "Straighten him out." What does that mean?

GABRIEL: Well, you know. Get his mind right. Change his thinking.

THE LORD: You mean, manipulate his thoughts till he does what's right?

GABRIEL: Right!

THE LORD: But that's out of the question. I created the human race with freedom of choice — "free will"— I think their theologians call it. I can't change the fact of free will, even if I wanted to. Which I don't.

GABRIEL: It seems to me it would make things a lot easier if you did.

THE LORD: And I tell you again, it's not possible. The human creatures would no longer be fully human. What else do you suggest?

GABRIEL:	Well, then, how about an exodus?
THE LORD:	A what?
GABRIEL:	An exodus. Let the children of Israel escape from all their troubles by leaving Egypt and going elsewhere.
THE LORD:	Now you're talking. We could lead them to a real nice place. To a land flowing with ... with milk and honey.
GABRIEL:	I like that! A land flowing with milk and honey. Has a real nice sound to it.
THE LORD:	How will we get them there? Maybe they won't want to go.
GABRIEL:	Of course they will. They'd be fools not to jump at the chance to leave Egypt.
THE LORD:	I wonder. It's been my experience that many people prefer the security of whatever in their lives holds them captive to the risk and uncertainty of freedom.
GABRIEL:	Then make them leave Egypt.
THE LORD:	But you forget. I can't force a man or a woman to do anything they do not choose to do.
GABRIEL:	Then send someone to persuade them, to lead them.
THE LORD:	My thoughts exactly. But who?
GABRIEL:	Well, he ought to be someone who can command respect. An important man, one who is ...
THE LORD:	Does it have to be a man? How about a woman?
GABRIEL:	Well ... I ... uh ... I personally have nothing against a woman, you understand.
THE LORD:	Oh yes, I understand, Gabriel.
GABRIEL:	I'm just not sure the children of Israel are quite ready to have a female lead them.

Still, if we found a woman with the right qualifications ...

THE LORD: What qualifications do you have in mind?

GABRIEL: For one thing, he ... or she ... should be someone who already has the confidence of the people. Then, of course, he's got to be good at public speaking ... a persuasive speaker. And he ...

THE LORD: Or she, Gabriel?

GABRIEL: Oh, right, right. Or "she." He or she ought to be experienced in administration.

THE LORD: All right. That's quite a list of qualifications. Do you know anyone who fits them?

GABRIEL: How about Eliab? He strikes me as just right for...

THE LORD: No, not him.

GABRIEL: Just like that ... no? All right, how about Caleb?

THE LORD: He's a good man, but not for this job.

GABRIEL: You want a woman, okay, what about Tirzah?

THE LORD: No.

GABRIEL: Dathan seems to have the qualifications that we...

THE LORD: Dathan? You can't be serious. Gabriel, you just don't have it when it comes to personnel work. Exactly what are your special abilities?

GABRIEL: *(pouting)* I think I do a pretty good job as an angel. *(trying to appear modest)* And folks tell me I have a flair for ... for ...

THE LORD: For what, Gabriel?

GABRIEL: For playing the trumpet.

THE LORD:	Really? I must have you play for me some time. One of these days I'm going to need a good trumpet player. But let's get back to a leader for the ... the exodus, I think you called it. What do you think of Moses?
GABRIEL:	Moses? Moses who? I've never heard of him.
THE LORD:	He fled from Egypt forty years ago after he had killed one of Pharaoh's men. He's been keeping sheep over in Midian.
GABRIEL:	That doesn't sound like a very good background for this kind of job, Lord.
THE LORD:	Nevertheless, he's the one I want. Let's go see him. *(They exit)*

Scene 2

(Moses enters and moves to center stage. He stops when he sees the "burning bush." The Lord and Gabriel enter, but Moses does not see them)

MOSES:	What is this? A bush that burns but is not consumed!
THE LORD:	Moses, Moses!
MOSES:	Here am I.
THE LORD:	Come no nearer. Take off your shoes, for the place on which you stand is holy ground. I am the God of your father, the God of Abraham, the God of Isaac, and the God of Jacob. *(Moses kneels and hides his face)*
Gabriel	Well, at least he shows a proper amount of respect.
THE LORD:	I tell you, Gabriel, this is the person I want. In fact, he's the only one who can do the job.

GABRIEL: I still don't know what you see in him. He looks like an ordinary sheepherder to me. And why do you need anyone? Why not just lead the people out of Egypt by yourself? Men ... and women ... are so undependable.

THE LORD: Undependable? Yes. But the fact remains that I designed human life to be in partnership with me. There are some things ... many things ... I cannot do on my own. I need the cooperation of the human creatures. They need me; I need them. And right now I need Moses.
(*Addresses Moses*) I have seen the affliction of my people who are in Egypt, and have heard their cry. I know their sufferings, and I mean to deliver them out of the hands of the Egyptians and bring them to a land rich and broad, a land flowing with milk and honey. (*Nods and smiles at Gabriel*) I will send you to Pharaoh to bring the children of Israel, my people, out of Egypt.

MOSES: Who am I that I should go to Pharaoh and bring the children of Israel out of Egypt?

GABRIEL: There, you see. He's scared. No self-confidence at all. I thought you said he was a man of faith.

THE LORD: (*Ignoring Gabriel*) Moses, fear not. I will be with you. And when you have brought the people out of Egypt, you will serve me upon this mountain.

MOSES: But if I go to the people and they ask me, "Who has sent you?" then what will I say?

GABRIEL: The impudence of this fellow! He dares to ask the Lord for some kind of identification. Oh Lordy, what an ignoramus!

THE LORD: Gabriel! I said you could abbreviate the long string of names with which you addressed me. But I do think "Lordy" is a bit too familiar. Do you catch my meaning?

GABRIEL:	*(repentant)* Yes, Lord God.
THE LORD:	*(To Moses)* I Am Who I Am. I Will Be Who I Will Be. Say this to the people of Israel: "I Am has sent me to you."
MOSES:	But they will not believe me. They will ask for a sign.
THE LORD:	I will give them signs aplenty. You will take water from the Nile and pour it upon the dry ground, and the water will be changed to blood upon the dry ground.
MOSES:	Lord God, I am a man with a wife and children. I have obligations to them.
THE LORD:	I will care for you and them while you do my work.
MOSES:	But, my Lord, I am not eloquent. I am slow of speech and of tongue.
GABRIEL:	*(Can contain himself no longer)* But we agreed we needed an articulate and persuasive speaker! Lord God, begging your pardon, but are you sure this is the right Moses? He just doesn't seem ...
THE LORD:	*(To Moses)* Who has made a man's mouth? Who makes him dumb or deaf or seeing or blind? Is it not I, the Lord? Now therefore, go, and I will be with your mouth and teach you what you shall speak.
MOSES:	Oh, my Lord, please send someone else.
GABRIEL:	I can't stand it. Lord, this guy is a loser. Now he's saying, "Let George do it." How often have we heard that before? What do you see in this man?
THE LORD:	Gabriel, I have told you that Moses is the one I have chosen. I know him better than he knows himself. The day will come when he will be hailed as the great deliverer, the giver of the Law. Without him, Israel will remain forever in bondage. I know well

enough his shortcomings. He is short-tempered and impulsive. He needs prodding. He is not a gifted speaker. But he has within him the spark of greatness, which, when I blow upon it, will become a fire like onto the fire in this bush. It is a fire which will consume all Egypt. Moses and I together are a match for any Pharaoh that's ever lived. *(To Moses)* Moses, your brother Aaron will be your voice. You and he will stand before Pharaoh and say this to him: "Thus says the Lord, 'Israel is my people, and I say to you, Let my people go that they may serve me.'"

MOSES: Lord, you are God. You are the Almighty One. Your word none can resist. The lion has roared; who will not fear? The Lord God has spoken; who can but prophesy?

THE LORD: Arise, Moses. I will be with you. Go in the peace and the might of God. *(Exit Moses)*

GABRIEL: I sure hope you're right about him. I still think Eliab has ...

THE LORD: Yes, Gabriel, I'm sure you do think Eliab is the right man for the job. Maybe that's why I'm the Lord and you're not. You know, I like this spot. It's so peaceful here. *(Notices Gabriel's feelings have been hurt)* Please don't take offense, Gabriel. I didn't mean to put you down. It's just that I call women and men to the tasks for which they are suited by their unique gifts. I'll tell you what. Let's go on back, and you go get your trumpet. I'm holding auditions for a very important upcoming event. Who knows? Maybe you're the right man for that job.

Who
Do You
Say
I Am?

PRODUCTION NOTES

As with all monologues, this one makes heavy demands on the actor. Besides the extended memorization required, the lack of interchange between characters means a dynamic performance is needed to engage the attention of the audience or congregation. In order to put some movement into the play, it is suggested that Simon alternate between standing, walking about, and sitting at appropriate intervals. A pitcher of water with a glass will give Simon something to do with his hands. Facial expression and gestures are essential in helping the person playing the part of Simon give life to the character. From what we can tell of the scriptures, Simon Peter was an impetuous, active man. Those qualities should come through in expression of the voice and body.

Simon's clothing can be the loose robe of his own time or it can be modern dress, according to the actor's or director's preference.

Suggested scripture text: Mark 8:27–38

A Monologue

SIMON PETER: My birth name is Simon ... Simon bar John, to be precise, which means simply, Simon son of John. You know me better by my given name, Peter. I say it is my given name because it was indeed given to me ... by Jesus himself. For a short time I was very proud of that name; as you may know, it means "rock." Then for a time the name embarrassed me, shamed me. I cringed whenever people called me Peter. And then, finally, I accepted the name again, not with pride this time, but with deep humility and gratitude. The story of how I came first to glory in my nickname, then to despise it, and finally to affirm it, is the story of my life.

I'd like to tell you some of my story. I'll explain why I want to tell it to you a bit later. For now, I will say only that my story isn't only about me; it is also about you. But I'm getting ahead of myself.

By the way, I must tell you that I am not comfortable in this time period you call the late twentieth century. It's not simply that your modern way of life is so much more complex and rapid than the life I lived in Galilee so many years ago. In time I suppose I could adjust to your pace (though to be honest, I'm rather glad I don't have to).

No, what causes me immense discomfort are the names of so many churches in this country and around the world. It's "Saint Peter's" here and there and everywhere it seems. The big one, of course, is over there in Rome; and maybe I should be gratified by the honor of the thing. But I'm not, not a bit. I find it terribly embarrassing and ... dare I say it? ... even blasphemous. It implies that I possessed some special kind of goodness, that I was an extra-special follower of my Lord, even that my life is a model for other believers. And my only response to such nonsense is to ask: doesn't anyone ever read the Gospels, for heaven's sake? The whole sorry record of my performance is all there for the world to see. Looking back on what I said and did, I can still scarcely believe that Jesus chose me to be one of his followers. And then, after I proved to be such a disaster, he still went on loving me and trusting me. I am amazed by it all even now, after all these years.

Of course, it didn't start out to be anything amazing at all. It began one day that was just like any other day. My brother Andrew and I were working on the shore of Lake Galilee. I've sometimes said my life began that day, and in one sense that's so. Up till then ... Well, my brother and I had a modest fishing operation; better than most, to tell the truth. I was comfortable. So when I looked up and saw this man standing there and heard him say, "Follow me," I cannot tell you for the life of me why I went with him. But I did; we both did. And our lives were never to be the same.

Don't misunderstand. It wasn't quite as dramatic and decisive as the Gospels make it sound. My brother and I had both heard about this Nazarene before he asked us to follow him. He'd come into Galilee preaching up a storm, had made quite an impression. I'd heard him a time or two myself. There was something about him that was ... well, compelling. And it was that quality about him we both responded to that day. Yes, it was an impulsive thing we did, leaving our nets that way; and many have wondered how we could have done it. All I can say is that had you been there that day and heard his words, seen his face, I think you would have come with us.

But, you see, we had no idea what was to come of it. We certainly did not think this was a lifetime adventure we were embarking on. For all we knew, "Follow me" meant simply going with him for the rest of that day. How were we to know there would be no going back to our fishing? We went with him that day and stayed with him the next and the next and the day after that until gradually, but surely, we were his disciples. We were in it all the way.

So we followed. And at first it was fantastic. I mean, I had never thought in terms of life being an exciting thing. Always before, there was work and sleep and a good meal and loving times with my wife and laughter and sport with friends. And there were hard times too, disappointment, even grief. But with Jesus, there was something new. He was always doing and saying the unexpected. What a thrill it was to watch him heal sick people, to drive out the unclean spirits. When he spoke, the people hung on his every word.

It was a heady experience for someone like me, I can tell you. It was intoxicating. Here I was, a country fisherman, the trusted follower of this man whose reputation was sweeping the countryside. Crowds flocked to him. We sometimes had to act like bodyguards to keep him from being overwhelmed by their adulation, their desperate attempts to get his attention so he would touch them, heal them.

It all went to my head much, as I have said, like strong wine. I got to thinking of myself as a pretty fine fellow. Jesus even singled out me and James and John as his closest comrades.

Added to all the wondrous things Jesus did was a certain sense of mystery in the air. I can't describe it exactly. Part of it was the danger. Many of the men who ran things in our land began to resent his popularity. Soon they were openly showing their contempt. Jesus did not back away from confronting them. We all sensed the rising danger. But that too can be exhilarating. Life lived on the edge has its own special kick. And Jesus reinforced the atmosphere of suspense by the mysterious parables he told. Those of us closest to him wondered why he so often asked the people he healed to keep it a secret.

It all came to a head on the day we were going to Caesarea Philippi. Almost casually Jesus asked us, "What are people saying about me? Who they do they say I am?" So we told him the scuttlebutt, how some were saying he was John the Baptist or one of the prophets. Then he asked, just as calmly, "What about you? Who do you say that I am?"

All at once it got very quiet. So quiet it seemed we had all stopped breathing. I think we sensed that this was it, this was the question we had all been waiting eagerly for and dreading at the same time. Because, you see, we didn't know who he was. That was the point. We knew he was somebody special, all right. It didn't take a genius to figure that out if you had seen him feed thousands with a few loaves or watched him pull the teeth of a Galilee night storm. But exactly who he was, that was a tough one. We really had no idea. What's more, we were half afraid to find out.

So how was it that I said what I said? How did I come to blurt out those words that marked the turning point in the whole business: "You are the messiah!"? I'll tell you the truth: I haven't the foggiest. It wasn't something I figured out on my own. I did not add two and two together and come up with four. No way! Even when I said it, even after I had said it, I can't say that I believed it truly. I was just as surprised as everyone else when it came out of my mouth.

But an even bigger surprise was still to come. Without so much as a nod of his head, Jesus began to say things we had never heard him say before. He told us what would happen to "the Son of man." And we knew he was referring to himself by that title. He said he would be rejected by the scribes and priests and would end up being tortured and killed. No riddles in what he said now, no parables that left us wondering what he was talking about. He told us flat out what was going to happen to him.

And it left us speechless. The horror of it was too much to comprehend. First, we could not accept that such a thing would ever happen to this man we had given our lives to. Second, if he was indeed the messiah, it was simply unthinkable that God's anointed one, the one our people had been praying and longing for so long, could suffer the fate that Jesus had just described. God's messiah, tortured and slaughtered? That simply wasn't possible.

Somehow I recovered first. It shames me now to say it, but I took Jesus to task. I told him what nonsense he was talking. I told him that he had it all wrong. My fears fueled my words; I poured out all kinds of things that, thank God, I can no longer remember. I blustered, I scolded, I pleaded.

Then it was his turn. With a fierceness I had rarely seen, he lit into me. He said I was opposing God. He said I was Satan. The shock of his words left me in a daze. It was only much later that I understood how my words must have been a temptation to him, the same kind of temptation he had faced alone in the wilderness when he could have chosen another way. He could have tried to live up to the people's expectation of the messiah, to come as conquering hero, to ride the crest of popularity for all it was worth. But he knew this was not God's way. So he turned his back on temptation. That's why he turned his back on me that day.

Now I understand. Because the temptation he faced is one we all face. Oh, never with as much at stake as when he faced it. But it is real enough for all that. Always we are tempted to take the easy way out, to suppose that we can dodge and weave and evade our way through life, without facing into the truth about ourselves. But it doesn't work that way. It's as Jesus told us that day. He said that being his disciple meant denying self and taking up a cross and following him.

Those of us with him that day weren't exactly thrilled at what he said, I can tell you. You must remember that the cross for us was not a lovely symmetrical symbol like the one you have up front here. No indeed. What the cross meant to us was shame and horror. Crucifixion was not only the most painful possible way to die, it was the symbol of the power of our hated Roman oppressors. It stood for the ultimate evil in our world. And here is Jesus saying that following him will mean bearing a cross.

No wonder we turned deaf ears to his words. No wonder that, right up to the very end, we kept denying that he would end up pinned to a cross like a helpless bug. If it's all the same to you, I will not dwell on the rest of my story. Because, to tell the truth, there on the road to Caesarea Philippi the whole tale of what my life was got told: the momentary courage, the denial of truth, the failure of nerve at the last.

You know most of the rest. How on the night before he was arrested I proudly told him that though everyone ran away I would stick by him. How when I followed him to the courtyard of the high priest while he was inside on trial for his life, I went to pieces at the taunting of a slave girl. I denied him three times. I will spare you the details of bitter self-recrimination.

Looking back on it now, I see that God was closer to me in those terrible moments than I ever knew. I faced the abyss. I had to acknowledge the awful truth about myself, that I could betray the very one who meant more to me than all else. I discovered I was capable of the worst that any human being can do. Have you faced that truth about yourself? If you haven't, I wonder if you really understand what the grace of God means. Believe me, it is no picnic when you see the worst about yourself. It was an agony for me. For a time, I felt forsaken by God.

But I wasn't. I know now that God was with me every step of the way, that the trial I faced was the only possible way I could ever fulfill the potential Jesus had seen in me from the very start. Somehow he knew me better than I knew myself. He saw past the bluster that camouflaged the mass of insecurities in my life. He had named me "Rock"; and for a time I thought that was a monstrous joke.

The turning point for me came after the resurrection. You can read about it in the fourth Gospel. Three times Jesus said to me, "Simon, son of John, do you love me?" How his words grieved me. How painfully obvious to me and the others that he called me not Peter, but Simon. Each time I answered, "Yes, Lord, you know that I love you." Each time he replied by telling me to feed his sheep. Three times, just as I had denied him three times. And then he said to me as he had said on that first day, "Follow me."

I knew then that he still loved me, that he had forgiven me. Even after my terrible denial, he wanted me to be his follower. And that's when my new life began. I don't want to talk about what happened to me after that. The facts tell only part of the story. The facts indicate that I became a courageous leader in the early church, that I won the respect of all believers. Tradition has it that I became the first bishop of Rome and eventually died for Jesus as he had died for me.

But all that isn't important. What is important about my story and why I have told it to you is the miracle that God can work in a person's life. If a blubbering coward like me could be turned into a rock, then that is to God's credit, not mine. I believe the living Christ can take the lowliest and least of us to accomplish unbelievable things. Oh, not as the world measures it. Success by God's definition is far different from the world's definition. Surely you know that by now.

What I'm trying to say to you is that the gospel really is good news. Christ not only died for you, he lives for you. And he will empower you to be his disciple to live with integrity and joy. All you need do is let him do for you what he did for me: make you over into what he wants you to become. For Christ's dear sake, let him.

The King Who Got Lost

PRODUCTION NOTES

The bad guys in the Bible hardly ever get to tell their side of the story. That is surely the case with one of the worst of the lot, Herod, the king who brings a note of terror to the beloved Christmas story.

In this play, which uses a "Meet the Press" format, Herod has the chance to set the record straight. The set for the play should include a table behind which the three reporters sit at a forty-five degree angle to the audience. Herod will sit facing them in a comfortable chair. Herod should be an older man; he should be dressed in royal garb, an expensive-looking robe, with a showy gold chain around his neck, etc. If costuming is a problem, Herod may wear a modern three-piece suit. In any case, he should come across as very much a product of his own time and place in history. The First Reporter serves as moderator.

Suggested scripture text: Matthew 2:1-18

CAST

FIRST REPORTER

SECOND REPORTER

THIRD REPORTER

HEROD

FIRST REPORTER:	*(Addressing audience)* We're fortunate to have with us today on Meet the Press none other than King Herod, the same Herod so familiar to us from the Christmas story. *(Addressing Herod)* Excellency, we're very happy you could join us for our session today.
HEROD:	Not at all. I'm happy to have the chance to tell my side of the story.
FIRST REPORTER:	Well then, let's get right to our questions. Terry, why don't you begin?
SECOND REPORTER:	Excellency, why were you so angry with the wise men when they didn't come back as you had asked them to? And why did you kill all the children in Bethlehem? If you don't mind my saying so, that seems like a barbaric thing to do.
HEROD:	Well, if you don't mind my saying so, I couldn't care less for your opinion. What do you know about being king? Anyway, I don't remember the event to which you're referring.
SECOND REPORTER:	You mean you actually forgot the mass murder of those children after the wise men came telling you about seeing the star?
HEROD:	The star? Oh yes, the star! Now I remember. That was a new twist, to be sure.
THIRD REPORTER:	What do you mean, "a new twist"?
HEROD:	A question like that just proves the point. You twentieth century people don't know anything about the business of being king. Very well, I'll tell you some things that may open your eyes a bit. First of all, do you know that I was a Jew myself? Many people think that, just because I was appointed by Rome to be king of Palestine, I was also a Roman. But actually my parents had converted to the Jewish religion.

THIRD REPORTER:	Did you practice your religion?
HEROD:	Nah. All that stuff about the righteousness and power of the Jewish God always struck me as so much nonsense. There really was only one power in my time.
FIRST REPORTER:	You mean ... Rome?
HEROD:	Rome. I always made sure my actions would keep Rome happy. It wasn't easy, you know, playing politics with such slippery characters as Mark Antony and Cleopatra and Augustus. I could tell you stories ... Anyway, I'm proud of my record of lasting 33 years as king in a time when everyone and his brother was out to get me. But let me get back to the point. You'll forgive an old man for rambling. The thing is, you can't imagine a worse bunch of subjects than those Jews. They were always trying to make trouble. I guess they were a bit upset because they thought I was betraying the nation and the religion by taking my orders from Rome. As if they would have been better off without Roman rule! Why, with all those hotheads running around, stirring up trouble, they'd have all killed each other if I hadn't been around to clamp down. I can't remember how many trouble-makers I had to have crucified. They just wouldn't learn.
SECOND REPORTER:	You have no regrets about the violent way you handled them?
HEROD:	None. I have only one regret in my life, and that is that I made such a mess of family affairs.
FIRST REPORTER:	The history books say you had several wives.
HEROD:	I had ten wives, if you must know. That was a few too many, even for a king to handle. (laughs)

It was bad enough with all the wives fighting among themselves, but add to that ten mothers-in-law, and you can see I had quite a problem. I had to get rid of a few wives and mothers-in-law too.

THIRD REPORTER: Got rid of?

HEROD: I had them executed ... or, in some cases, murdered.

THIRD REPORTER: You don't seem apologetic about it.

HEROD: What is there to apologize for? They were plotting to have me assassinated, so their sons could take my place. I had to kill some of my sons for the same reason. I had quite a few of my most trusted aides liquidated too, because they started getting ideas. It was either them or me in every case. Being king is a pretty bloody business. But the record shows that the country had no really bad wars through my reign, despite all my family trouble.

FIRST REPORTER: You were going to tell us about the star...

HEROD: Oh yes, the star. Well, my Jewish subjects had the idea that their God was going to send them a king. He would come on the scene and then set up his own kingdom. They called him the messiah. Naturally, I thought it was just superstition. But the trouble was, they took it seriously. So whenever some hothead started trouble somewhere, right away they would all get excited. "Oh, it's the messiah," they would say. Of course, it never was, but it caused me a lot of trouble. I always saw to it that such problems never got out of hand. I nipped them in the bud, so to speak.

SECOND REPORTER: But about the star...

HEROD: I'm getting to that. The star business came at a very bad time for me. A few of my sons had been plotting to get rid of me, and I had just managed to get things under control again when these foreigners came to Jerusalem and began asking some stupid questions about a star. As if I spent my time watching the stars all night!

SECOND REPORTER: Why didn't you just tell them to leave?

HEROD: I was ready to do just that until they said this star meant that a king of the Jews had been born and they had come to worship him. That got my attention, all right.

THIRD REPORTER: So you believe in messages from the stars?

HEROD: Astrology? Don't be ridiculous! I just didn't want these strange-looking foreigners spreading the word that a king of the Jews had been born. If such a rumor got started, I'd have a terrible mess on my hands. The news would get across the country in no time, and then there would be uprisings and riots. Everyone would be saying, "It's the messiah," all over again. So I figured out a way to keep things under control. I decided to play along with these so-called wise men.

FIRST REPORTER: So that's why you called in the religious leaders to tell you what the scriptures said about where the messiah would be born?

HEROD: Right! You catch on fast! I told the Jewish holy men that I wanted to learn more about the scriptures. It was a good public relations maneuver, and they fell for it. I asked them where the prophets predicted the messiah would appear. They said in Bethlehem, and they quoted some scripture to prove it. I had those foreigners listening in on this conference, and when I was alone with them again, I really went into my act. I pretended to be greatly interested in their search, asked all kinds of questions, and then sent them to Bethlehem with instructions to report to me when they found the king.

THIRD REPORTER: Didn't you think they might suspect your real motives?

HEROD: Nah. They were as innocent as babes themselves. They never suspected a thing. I figured it this way. If they never found this king—and I doubted they would, to say the least—no harm would be done. People would regard them as fools. If they did pick a baby to call a king, I would wait until they left the country and then ... take measures.

THIRD REPORTER: You mean ...?

HEROD: Yes. But as it turned out, the foreigners tricked me. Through some informers, I learned they had vanished. So rumors were already starting to fly. The only thing I could do was to have all the male children in and around Bethlehem disposed of. That pretty well settled the issue. If there was a king, he sure got lost in a hurry. *(laughs)*

FIRST REPORTER: And that settled matters?

HEROD: Oh yes. The rumors stopped, and I could turn my attention to important matters.

SECOND REPORTER: You seem to treat the whole thing rather offhandedly. It might interest you to know that those children were "disposed of," as you put it, in vain.

HEROD: What do you mean?

SECOND REPORTER: Well, the king the Jews were looking for, their messiah, turned out to be quite different from the king they had expected. He wasn't a military figure, and he certainly never would have threatened to take your throne.

HEROD: You don't say! Well, things work out strangely sometimes. By the way, I noticed on my way here that there are decorations and lights everywhere. Is there a holiday going on?

THIRD REPORTER: Yes. It's Christmas.

HEROD: Christmas? What's that?

THIRD REPORTER: It's a celebration for the birth of a king.

HEROD: A king? Is he king of your country?

SECOND REPORTER: No. He was born about 2,000 years ago, during your reign. In fact, he is the one those wise men were searching for?

HEROD: You don't say! And what nation did he become king of?

FIRST REPORTER: He did not have a kingdom in the sense you're familiar with.

HEROD: Then what was his kingdom like?

SECOND REPORTER: It's a kingdom of peace, of good will, of love among all people. It is a kingdom in which people's lives are fulfilled and joyful, a kingdom where justice and freedom reign.

HEROD: (scornfully) And where did such a kingdom exist?

THIRD REPORTER: Not in a country, but in the lives of people who believe in and follow this king. These people still live in this kingdom.

HEROD: Which people?

THIRD REPORTER: The ones called Christians.

HEROD: Oh yes. Christians. I've heard of them. There are quite a few in this country, aren't there? Then your king, whoever he is, is very lucky. He wouldn't have the problems I did: of crime and jealousies and poverty. Now I can see why you got so upset about the killing of infants. Obviously your country would do all it could to see that

babies and children had healthy, produc-
tive lives. Right?

FIRST REPORTER: Well, that's not quite the way it is. Unfor-
tunately, most of those problems you had
when you were king are still with us. Most
Christians don't take their faith all that
seriously.

HEROD: I see. Sounds to me as if that king got lost
again.

FIRST REPORTER: Yes, Excellency, I'm afraid it does.

Record of Use

That Your Days May Be Long

1. Date: _____
   Event: _____
   Cast: Michael Soan: _____
             Daphne Carnes: _____
             Geroge Harding: _____
             Mary McClain: _____
             Kathrine Daniels: _____
             Peter Kravek: _____
             Old Woman: _____
             Child: _____

2. Date: _____
   Event: _____
   Cast: Michael Soan: _____
             Daphne Carnes: _____
             Geroge Harding: _____
             Mary McClain: _____
             Kathrine Daniels: _____
             Peter Kravek: _____
             Old Woman: _____
             Child: _____

Pharaoh Decides

1.   Date: _____

     Event: _____

     Cast: Pharaoh's Daughter: _____

              Setimose: _____

              Tutamon: _____

              Pharaoh: _____

2.   Date: _____

     Event: _____

     Cast: Pharaoh's Daughter: _____

              Setimose: _____

              Tutamon: _____

              Pharaoh: _____

After the Whale

1.   Date: _____

     Event: _____

     Cast: Stage Manager: _____

              The Ninevite: _____

              Jonah: _____

2.   Date: _____

     Event: _____

     Cast: Stage Manager: _____

              The Ninevite: _____

              Jonah: _____

The Millionaires

1. Date: _____
   Event: _____
   Cast: George: _____
         Mary Jane: _____
         Narrator: _____
2. Date: _____
   Event: _____
   Cast: George: _____
         Mary Jane: _____
         Narrator: _____

Lazarus Unbound

1. Date: _____
   Event: _____
   Cast: Lazarus: _____
         Mark Callis: _____
2. Date: _____
   Event: _____
   Cast: Lazarus: _____
         Mark Callis: _____

A Story

1. Date: _____
    Event: _____
    Cast: Narrator: _____
               René/René: _____
               Ant: _____
               Flower: _____
               Tree: _____
               Pebble: _____

2. Date: _____
    Event: _____
    Cast: Narrator: _____
               René/René: _____
               Ant: _____
               Flower: _____
               Tree: _____
               Pebble: _____

Right Man for the Job

1. Date: _____
    Event: _____
    Cast: The Lord: _____
               Gabriel: _____
               Moses: _____

2. Date: _____
    Event: _____
    Cast: The Lord: _____
               Gabriel: _____
               Moses: _____

Who Do You Say I Am?

1. Date: _____
    Event: _____
    Cast: Simon Peter: _____
2. Date: _____
    Event: _____
    Cast: Simon Peter: _____

The King Who Got Lost

1. Date: _____
    Event: _____
    Cast: First Reporter: _____
            Second Reporter: _____
            Third Reporter: _____
            Herod: _____
2. Date: _____
    Event: _____
    Cast: First Reporter: _____
            Second Reporter: _____
            Third Reporter: _____
            Herod: _____

Request
for
Permission to Perform

make a photocopy of this form and send it to:
faithQuest
1451 Dundee Avenue
Elgin, IL 60120

I (We) request permission to perform the play:

_____

from the collection That Your Days May Be Long: And Other Religious Dramas (by Kenneth L. Gibble). Performances will take place on the following date(s):

_____

at the following location(s):

_____

In order to hold rehearsals we:

    ☐ (option 1) request permission to photocopy the play for script copies

    ☐ (option 2) request that you ship us ____ copies of the book at the special 50% script discount ($5.48 ea). My (Our) check for $_____ is enclosed with this form.

name	_____
institution	_____
address	_____
city, state, zip	_____

once a copy of this form has been sent to the publisher permission is given
    • to copy the indicated play in this book for scripts
    • to perform the play

no royalty payment is required